Four Cheshire Townships
in the 18th Century

6·15

Our wise Forefathers would express
Ev'n Sensibility in Dress:
The modern Race delight to show
What Folly in Excess can do.

What is this my Son Tom.

The honest Farmer, come to Town,
Can scarce believe his Son his own,
If thus the Taste continues Here,
What will it be another Year?

London, Published by M. Darly &c. &c.

Plate 1: *'What is this my Son Tom'*. This caricature by Mary Darly of the hairstyle of 1771 also illustrates that it was not unusual for a smart young tradesman or merchant to have a bucolic father.

CHARLES F. FOSTER

Four Cheshire Townships in the 18th Century

Arley, Appleton, Stockton Heath and Great Budworth

——

ARLEY HALL PRESS

First published 1992 by the Arley Hall Press, Northwich, Cheshire, CW9 6NB
(Tel. 0565-777 231 or 284)

ISBN 0 9518382 0 2

Designed by Peter Ballard

Acknowledgements

This essay has been produced in conjunction with the Historic Society of Lancashire
and Cheshire and will appear in the *Transactions* of the Society in 1992.
I am most grateful to the joint Editors for all their help.
   I would also like to thank my friend James Barfoot for creating the maps from the
eighteenth- and nineteenth-century originals.

Typeset in Ehrhardt by Alan Sutton Publishing Limited
Printed and bound at the Bath Press, Bath, Avon

Contents

MAPS

PLATES

I

Sir Peter Warburton's Estate
and his Papers

In 1743 Sir Peter Warburton, 4th Baronet, inherited the Arley estate, Cheshire. In 1745 he married Lady Elizabeth Stanley, eldest daughter of the 11th Earl of Derby, and brought her to Arley, where they lived together for the next twenty-nine years, bringing up their family, which consisted of a son, Sir Peter, 5th Bt, and five daughters of whom only three survived to adult life. Arley Hall had not been inhabited by the head of the family since the 1st Bt, Sir George, died in 1676. His eldest son, Sir Peter, 2nd Bt, had married a Hertfordshire heiress in 1673 and for the next seventy years he and his son George, 3rd Bt, preferred a London house and a country place near Hitchin to the ancestral Cheshire estate. But 1743 was the start of a new regime. Sir Peter reorganized the farms and enclosed the commons; he repaired and modernized Arley Hall and built new mills and farmhouses. He became during the 1750s, in effect but not in name, the chairman of the Weaver Navigation[1] and presided over a thorough modernization of that waterway which allowed Cheshire salt to capture the markets of the whole of northern Europe. He employed a series of trained accountants who organized an efficient office with detailed accounting procedures and well-kept files. By good fortune, his office papers have descended to us almost intact. Together with less comprehensive papers from before and after his time, these archives form the basis of this study,[2] which is a social survey of the people who lived around Arley in the 1740s – who they were, what they did and how much money they had.

Arley Hall lies in the township (or civil parish as it is now known) of Aston by Budworth (Map 1). To the south and west lies the village and township of Great Budworth in which the Warburtons had been the main freeholders since 1200. To the north-west is Crowley, which, despite it being so close to their house, the family had never owned. Beyond that is Appleton, where the Warburtons had been lords of the manor and the principal landowners since the early thirteenth century. These four townships are the subject of this book: Aston by Budworth (2,957 acres), Great Budworth (903 acres), Crowley (1,400 acres) and Appleton (3,422 acres). When Sir Peter inherited in 1743 he found that he had the following lands and income in three of these townships, as well as lands in five other townships, as Table 1 shows.

TABLE 1   *Sir Peter Warburton's estate, c. 1740–1750*[3]

	Approx statute acres	*Income £*
Aston by Budworth		
The Home Farm around Arley Hall	393	in kind 215
The remainder of the demesne land let to 14 tenants paying full annual or rack rents (Appendix 2.12)	824	424
32 tenants on three-life leases (Appendix 2.2)	730	42
Great Budworth		
33 tenants on three-life leases (Appendix 2.5)	468	35
Appleton		
43 tenants on three-life leases (Appendices 2.8 and 2.10)	1,443	50
Three farms let at rack rents	341	150
Sutton Weaver		
One farm let at rack rent	257	170
27 tenants on three life-leases	882	44
Warburton		
One farm let at rack rent	301	241
63 tenants on three-life leases	1,451	65
Lymm		
27 tenants on three-life leases	328	11
Marthall[4]		
One farm at rack rent	about 1,200	44
30 tenants on three-life leases		35
Pulford		
20 tenants on three-life leases	991	37
Mills, quarries, wharfs and warehouses		111
	Total 9,609	1,674

A striking feature of this list is that the income per acre he derived from the tenants paying full annual or rack rents is so much larger than that derived from the three-life leases. Three-life leases were standard practice

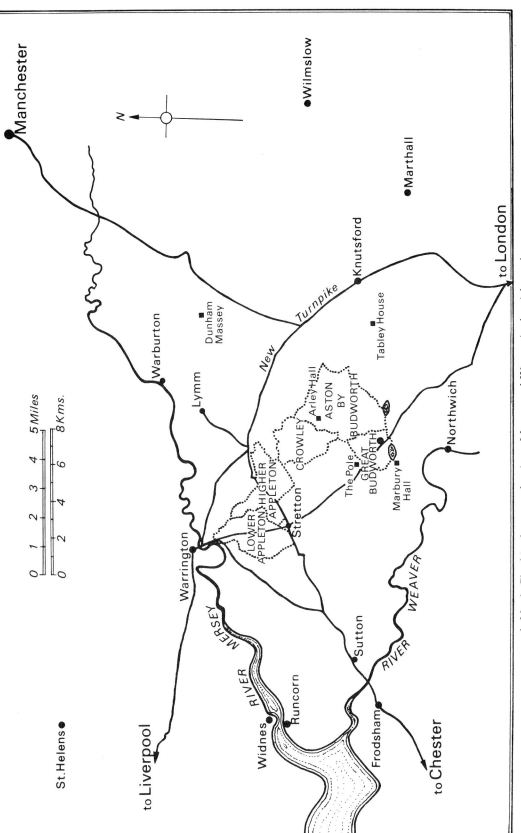

1. North Cheshire between the rivers Mersey and Weaver in the eighteenth century.

on all old landed estates in Cheshire and Lancashire from the middle of the sixteenth to the end of the eighteenth centuries. A tenant bought a lease of his farm at a very small rent, called 'old rent', for the lives of three named individuals, frequently children, for a fine of about twelve times the annual value. For example, a farm worth £10 a year would cost £120 and a rent of 10s. a year. When a life died, tenants could add another life which normally cost two years' value for one life and five years' value for two lives. Tenants could buy and sell these three-life leases. Thus in addition to the income in Table 1, Sir Peter would receive fines for adding lives to leases; these fines, sales of timber, and of bark used for tanning leather, probably totalled between £500 and £1,000 p.a., so that he could usually reckon on a total gross income of about £2,500 a year.

To understand what such an income meant in the eighteenth century, it is necessary to look at what other people had. There were probably between 300 and 500 families in England with a larger income than the Warburtons. Five or six of these may have been Cheshire families – Cholmondeley, Grosvenor, Booth and Crewe, for example – but marriages and deaths frequently altered the pecking order. Many of the richest families were headed by a nobleman, of whom there were about 180 in England, and about ten peers had incomes as high as £20,000 p.a.[5] At the other end of the spectrum, the weekly time-sheets for the Arley estate in 1750 show that it was paying the men on the home farm 8d. a day in the six winter months and 10d. a day in summer. They worked six days a week, so a full year's work came to £11 14s. 0d. Women normally earned 5d. a day, but those who could reap the harvest received 10d. like the men. Other occupations ranged around this. Mr Riley, the tailor, asked 8d. a day all the year (£10 8s. 0d. p.a.); carpenters, bricklayers and plumbers varied from 1s. 0d. to 1s. 6d. a day depending on their skills (from £15 14s. 0d. to £22 16s. 0d. p.a.). Thomas Howard, the builder, charged 2s. 6d. a day or £39 a year and professional men like lawyers and surveyors thought in terms of 5s. to 10s. a day (£80–£160 p.a.). To keep the money values in this study in perspective it may be useful to regard the basic wage for a fit adult male around Arley in 1750 as £12 a year and to consider that a lawyer earning £60 a year or a freeholder with £60 a year clear rent from his farm had five times as much as a manual worker.

II

The Social Revolution after c.1750

In the 1870s around 95% of the 8,682 acres in our four townships was owned by five squires.[6] The Warburtons had nearly 6,000 acres. The two banking families of Parr and Lyon, whose Parr's Bank in Warrington was merged with the Westminster Bank in 1918,[7] had created estates around Appleton Hall and Grappenhall Heyes. There were the Leighs in Great Budworth and the Leicesters (Lords de Tabley) in Aston. All these landowners rented most of their land to farmers and smallholders on seven- or fourteen-year leases at rack rents. There was a large income gap between these five great families and the rest of the rural community. This was in sharp contrast to the position in the 1740s. Table 2 summarizes the number of property-owners in our four townships.[8] Apart from the three

TABLE 2   *Number of property-owners in the four townships in the 1740s*

	Major landowners (See note 1)	*Freeholders* (see notes 2, 3, 4)	*Sir Peter Warburton's three-life leaseholders*	*Other landlords' three-life leaseholders*
Aston	3	4	32	10
Appleton Lower Town	1	24	17	–
Appleton Higher Town	1	11	30	–
Great Budworth	2	6	33	10
Crowley	–	17	–	–
Totals	3	62	112	20

Source: Appendices 2.1–2.11.[8]

Notes:
1. There were only three major landowners in total: Sir Peter Warburton; Sir Peter Leicester; executors of Sir Samuel Daniel.
2. John Egerton, esq., was the only freeholder with land in more than one township. He is included here with freeholders, not major landowners, because his land was probably not being let on three-life leases.
3. A small number of people who have lands in more than one category are counted twice – e.g. James Birchall, freeholder in Crowley and leaseholder in Aston.
4. About two-thirds of the freeholders had bought their estates since 1700.

TABLE 3 *Summary of area and annual value of lands by type of owner*

Property-owner	ASTON Statute acres	ASTON Annual value £	GREAT BUDWORTH Statute acres	GREAT BUDWORTH Annual value £	APPLETON Lower Town Statute acres	APPLETON Lower Town Annual value £	APPLETON Higher Town Statute acres	APPLETON Higher Town Annual value £	CROWLEY Statute acres	CROWLEY Annual value £	Totals Statute acres	Totals %	Totals Annual Value £	Totals %
Freeholders	258	149	276	167	828	420	440	214	1343	753	3145	40	1703	39
Sir P. Warburton's demesne and rack rents	1217	640	–	–	124	48	217	98	–	–	1558	20	786	18
Sir P. Warburton' three-life leaseholders	730	525	468	341	491	240	952	439	–	–	2641	34	1545	36
Other gentry's three-life leaseholders	381	266	56	52	–	–	–	–	–	–	437	6	318	7
	2586	1580	800	560	1443	708	1609	751	1343	753	7781	100	4352	100
Commons and roads	220		70		–		240		57		587			
Total	2806		870				3292		1400		8368			
Ordnance Survey	2957		903				3422		1400		8682			

Notes:
1. All figures have been rounded.
2. Source: Appendices 2.1–2.12.
3. I am not able to account for the deficiency in acres between the eighteenth-century surveys and the Ordnance Survey. My figures are based on adding up some thousand individual field areas in the three 'Warburton' manors, and so small errors could multiply. There seems a tendency for old measurements to grow – as if old surveyors did not measure to the centre of boundary ditches. For example, Sir Peter Leicester has 357 acres in Aston in his survey of 1716, but 406 in the tithe map of 1836, and I know of 25 at most that he acquired between those dates. The Crowley figures are nineteenth-century.

major landowners there were sixty-two freeholders and 132 three-life leaseholders. In Table 3 it can be seen that the sixty-two freeholders had 40% of the land by acreage and 39% by annual value. See Appendix I for a description of the sources of these annual value figures. Sir Peter Warburton had 20% of the acreage that he was either occupying himself or letting to rack-rent tenants. The remaining 40% was in the hands of three-life leaseholders. Table 4 shows a calculation of the approximate capital value of the land at this period. Sir Peter Warburton had 36% – about half derived from his interest in the land occupied by these three-life leaseholders and the other half from his own and his rack-rented land. The sixty-two freeholders had 39% and the 132 three-life leaseholders had 21%, the remaining 4% being the other two large landowners' share of the 437 acres which they were letting on three-life leases. So the position in the 1740s was that 61% of the land by capital value was owned by 194 families and only 39% by great landowners. There was evidently a social revolution in the district between 1750 and 1870, and when we examine

TABLE 4 *The capital value of the land in the four townships in the 1740s*

		Annual value (see Note 1)	Multiplier (see Notes 2 & 3)	Capital value	%
		£		£	
Freeholders		1,703	25	42,575	39 Freeholders
Sir P. Warburton demesne and rack rents		786	25	19,650	36 Sir Peter Warburton
Sir. P. Warburton	freeholder's share	1,545	$12\frac{1}{2}$	19,312	
Three-life leaseholders	leaseholder's share		$12\frac{1}{2}$	19,312	21 three-life leaseholders
Other gentry	leaseholder' share	318	$12\frac{1}{2}$	3,975	
three-life leaseholders	freeholders' share		$12\frac{1}{2}$	3,975	4 Other gentrey
	Totals	4,319	25	108,799	100

Notes:
1. Annual values are the totals from Table 3. See Appendix 1 for sources of annual values.
2. Investors require a return on their money which is normally measured as a 'rate of interest'. In the 18th century the rate of interst on land and government bonds varied between $2\frac{1}{2}$% and 5% per annum. Another way of looking at this is to describe the capital value (say 100) as 20 times the interst (5%) or 40 times $2\frac{1}{2}$%. 25 times the annual value was a common price for a freehold farm.
3. The normal price for a three-life lease was about $12\frac{1}{2}$ times the annual value. In this way, the freeholders right to get the land back at the end of the lease was valued at $12\frac{1}{2}$ times, which was the other half of 25 times.

the leases and deeds we discover that most of it occurred between 1750 and 1830.[9] If we look backwards we find that there were similar numbers of three-life leaseholders round 1600[10] and that many of the freeholds can be traced back to the thirteenth and fourteenth centuries.[11] In the 1740s we stand, therefore, on the brink: the old rural society that had its roots in the Middle Ages was to be destroyed within a century.

It is the object of this study to examine the social structure of these four townships in the 1740s. Appendices 2.1–2.11 list all the property-owners, with the modern address of each property, its area and its annual value in the 1740s. I have added notes which briefly describe how and when many of the owners acquired their land and what their occupations and family circumstances were at the time.

III

Representative Property-owners Described

THE MAJOR LANDOWNERS

Of the three major landowners identified in Table 2, Sir Peter Warburton's estate of about 9,600 acres and his income of about £2,500 p.a. have been described in detail. Sir Peter Leicester of Tabley Hall had an estate of similar value but with a different history. The Leicester family had lived at Lower Tabley since the thirteenth century; they had a home farm there and the rest of the demesne was let to rack-rent tenants. Although the remainder of their north Cheshire estate was only half the size of the Warburtons' it was scattered over fifteen townships. Most of their tenants had three-life leases and there were eight of them on 357 acres in Aston and ten on fifty-six acres in Great Budworth. In 1728, Meriel, the Leicester heiress, married Sir John Byrne, Bt, so that when their son inherited both estates in 1742 and changed his name to Leicester, the Byrne lands in Yorkshire and Sligo roughly doubled the size and value of the Leicester estate.[12] The other major landowner of Table 2, Sir Samuel Daniel, had an old estate based on Over Tabley when he died without a male heir in 1726 and it passed to trustees for his daughter's children. It included just two three-life leaseholders on twenty-four acres in Aston.[13]

14

The sixty-two freeholders provide a sample of the freeholders of north Cheshire in the 1740s. Table 5 divides them into six groups; leaving the unknowns aside, examples of families in each of the five occupational groups are described.

TABLE 5   *The annual value of lands held by various occupational groups among the freeholders*

Township	Gentry normally called esquire	Professionals i.e. Lawyers and Doctors	Churchmen	Businessmen	Gentlemen and working farmers	Unknown or others	Total value
	£ p.a.	£ p.a.	£ p.a.	£ p.a.	£ p.a.	£ p.a.	£ p.a.
Aston	75				74		149
Great Budworth	69		4	44	50		167
Appleton Lower Town	99	27	40	21	174	59	420
Appleton Higher Town	70		74		54	16	214
Crowley	115	97	46	216	242	37	753
Totals	428	124	164	281	594	112	1703
%	25	7	10	16	35	7	100

Sources: Appendix 1 for valuation, and Appendices 2.1, 2.4, 2.7, 2.9, and 2.11

(a) The gentry

A quarter (by value) of the land owned by freeholders was in the hands of the gentry. These were usually people with smaller estates than the Warburtons and Leicesters but having more than one or two farms. They were normally addressed in eighteenth-century society as esquire. Some owed their social position at least partly to marriage. Thomas Slaughter became brother-in-law to Sir Peter Warburton when he married his sister Ann in 1739. In 1749 they moved to a large house in Chester where they brought up their family. They never invested the money they received from Sir George Warburton, 3rd Bt, in a landed estate but more adventurously sank it in a mining venture in North Wales. They sold the Budworth estate, 109 acres worth £90 p.a.,[14] to the Hon. John Smith Barry (son of the Earl of Barrymore) who wished to be near his elder brother Richard who lived

15

in Marbury Hall. John Barry built Belmont and lived in it for the rest of his life but never owned more than 160 acres around his new house.[15] His income was probably derived from a share in his father's estate and his wife's inheritance in Essex.

The importance of marriage and male heirs to successful gentry families is again illustrated by the case of John Egerton. He was the younger son of the Revd Philip Egerton of Oulton and married Elizabeth Brock of Upton, near Chester. Her father had married Elizabeth Gregg of Bradley Hall in Appleton (157 acres put at £70 p.a.), a small but old estate that the Greggs had owned since at least the sixteenth century. Both ladies proved to be heiresses and from John Egerton these lands passed to his grandson who inherited the baronetcy from the other branch of the family and so became in 1814 Sir John Grey Egerton, Bt, of Egerton and Oulton.

Thomas Walton, who owned Litley Farm in Aston (135 acres, valuation £75 p.a.), is a mysterious figure who lived with the 2nd Earl of Warrington at Dunham Massey. He had £15,000 in cash and securities as well as several farms when he died in 1755. In an extraordinary document dated Christmas Day 1750, the Earl denied at length that he was the father of Miss Mary Walton 'the legitimate daughter of my servant Thomas Walton'. The latter bequeathed Litley Farm to the Earl's grandson, the Hon. Booth Grey.[16]

Another strand of gentry is represented by two families, Rutter of Moore Hall (west of Appleton) and Eaton of The Pole, Antrobus. Richard Rutter had inherited 172 acres in Crowley valued at £96 p.a. as well as lands in Moore, where he lived, and in Hatton and Latchford. In all he probably had about 1,000 acres, all let on full annual rents totalling some £400–£500 per annum. When he died in 1757 he left the whole estate to his daughter, who was still a child. He expressed the wish that his widow would bring her up in the main house until she was twenty-one and took possession. He gave his wife an annuity of £60 a year and provided that she could then move into two rooms in John Caldwell's farmhouse in Moore, which he had lately purchased and fitted up for his sister, who, however, had died before she could long enjoy them.[17] The fortunes of widows is a topic to which we will return. George Eaton of The Pole, Antrobus, was the largest freeholder in Appleton with 223 acres valued at £96 p.a. This land was mostly in two large farms, The Hurst and Shepcroft, which probably came to his family through marriage at the end of the seventeenth century. He built a new farmhouse at Shepcroft in 1731 and recorded his name and the date on a plaque which is still to be seen (Plate 2). His family had been at The Pole since at least the early seventeenth century and with the land there his total estate was probably between 500 and 1,000 acres, producing an income of £250–£500 p.a. He was on friendly terms with the Warburtons and was a trustee for old Sir George in 1739 and a fellow executor with Sir Peter for Admiral Hore in 1762. His sister married Richard Selby, vicar of Great Budworth (1741–87), in 1747. The vicar had an income in 1778, as he informed Christ Church, Oxford, the patron of the living, of £91 10s. a year.[18]

Plate 2: Great Shepcroft, Appleton Lower Town, built in 1731 by George Eaton as the house for this large tenanted farm of 113 acres. Compare Plates 3, 4 and 5.

(b) The professions

Another important figure in Budworth society in the 1740s came from the smallest group in Table 5; professional men – lawyers and doctors – had only 7% of the freehold land. Hamlet Yate can have only just qualified in the law when, in 1689, aged about 18,[19] he was appointed steward of the Arley estate. He was probably the son of a Warburton leaseholder and this connection got him the job, which he held for the next 44 years. As was the custom of the time, he had his own legal practice as well as working for the Warburtons. Yate seems to have lived in Arley Hall in the 1690s when his own children were born but around 1705 he built at Aston Park, where there was only 'an old kitchen and two or three bays of outbuilding', the house substantially as it remains today (Plate 3). While he was living there, his eldest daughter Ann married the head of a neighbouring gentry family, the Revd William Egerton Leigh of West Hall, High Legh.[20] By 1712 Hamlet Yate was rich enough to buy the freehold of the farm (109 acres) now known as Garland Hall.[21] With other smaller areas that he bought later he had by the 1740s accumulated 137 acres in Crowley worth £77 p.a. He also bought the two best Warburton leaseholds in Great Budworth – 131 acres worth another £77 p.a. – and another leasehold in Marthall[22] worth £45, so his total landed income was £199. His legal business, which consisted in the 1720s and 1730s of an office with pupils and clerks, must have brought in, with the Arley fees, at least another £100, perhaps £200. So he may well have had an annual income of £300 to £400 – enough to feel on equal terms with George Eaton. Indeed, as the local representative of Sir George Warburton, M.P. for the county in 1702–5 and 1710–22, he may well have felt his power and influence to be greater. But in 1732 Thomas Marsh, a leaseholder in Warburton, complained to Sir George about Mr Yate. Sir George sent a consultant, Mr Edward Lawrence, whose report on what he found survives.[23] Apparently Mr Yate had increased Thomas Marsh's fine for adding a life from £22 to £34 and asked £1 for himself which he had called Sir George's money. Sir George was reported to be very angry. Mr Yate was summoned to London (where he stayed at Mr Weekley's, tobacconist, near St Dunstan's church in Fleet Street) and his accounts for the previous 20 years were examined, after which he was sacked. The quarrel was so bitter that Mr Yate handed over to his successor, Francis Bartholomew, only the formal leases, a few rentals and the manor court records. Many letters and papers about Arley were found in his office twenty years later and were destroyed by his executors. He had to leave Aston Park and he went to live in his leasehold, the Old Hall in Great Budworth, with his unmarried daughter Mary. Perhaps the settlement with Sir George was expensive or he may have had to pay Egerton Leigh his wife's portion. Whatever the reason, in 1737 he mortgaged Garland Hall for £1,500. After he died in 1750 his daughter was unable to pay the interest so that by the time she sold the property in 1752 for £2,280, the mortgage amounted to £1,979 and she was left with only £300. She lived on in the Old Hall for the rest of her life but when she died in 1768 there cannot have been much left of what must have appeared an ample fortune in 1730.

By contrast, Dr Bent of Shrewsbury was but a transient freeholder in Appleton. In 1743 his father, a malt merchant of Warrington, bought a farm which the doctor sold in the late 1750s to Matthew Lyon.[24]

(c) Churchmen

Churchmen owned 10% by value of the freeholders' land in our sample. We have just seen, in the Leighs of West Hall, High Legh, that old gentry families were one source of clerics. The Revd Thomas Moss, who owned 127 acres in Appleton Higher Town valued at £74 in 1744, came from a

Plate 3: Aston Park, built by Hamlet Yate between 1705 and 1715 – 'a house fit for any gentleman'.

different background. His grandfather, who had acquired this land, his father and his elder brother were all successful woollen cloth merchants in Manchester. The grandfather, James, may have been related to a widow Moss who had a freehold in Appleton in 1666, and that may be the reason he agreed to lend £400 in 1678 to Thomas Millington, gentleman, on a mortgage of his Green Lane Farm, Appleton. Over the next five years Moss bought most of the ancient Millington freehold. The young Millington son, deprived of his inheritance, went to London and established a silk dyeing business near St Martin-in-the-Fields. It was not until 1707 that he severed the last link with Appleton and sold out to John, son of James Moss. John Moss continued his father's business so successfully that he was able to acquire the manor of Little Bolton and Tong, to build a chapel there and to buy tithes with which to endow it. When he died in 1729 he left his business and his manor to his eldest son and his Appleton property and other lands to his second son Thomas, born 1712, who entered the Church via Brasenose College, Oxford (M.A. 1738), and in due course became a fellow of the collegiate church of Manchester. In 1749 Thomas married Sarah, daughter of Thomas Parker, another prosperous Manchester merchant who was able to give a portion of £2,000 with his daughter, who in turn secured a jointure of £60 p.a. from her new husband. Although he had become a man of God, Thomas still bore the imprint of his business upbringing. He added to his Appleton farmland a lease from the Arley estate of the Saracen's Head Inn and malt kiln at Wilderspool and seems to have been involved with the Hart and Lyon families in the establishment of a brewery there. He also assisted his brother in a large property development on college lands in Manchester called The Parsonage.[25]

The other clerical freeholder was an absentee whose holding in Appleton is nevertheless an interesting example of the connections between land ownership and trade which seem to have characterized this area. The Revd Thomas Leigh was rector of Stoke Bruern in Northamptonshire, but the second son of George Leigh, esquire, of nearby Oughtrington, Lymm, Cheshire. George's sister Mary had married in 1660 into the Patten family, whose Bank Quay was the first terminal for ocean-going ships at Warrington. The mercantile connections were continued when the Revd Thomas Leigh's sister married the eminent Liverpool merchant William Clayton, mayor of the town in 1689 and one of its M.P.s from then until his death in 1715. It was the children of this marriage who received the Revd Thomas Leigh's legacies of between £4,000 and £5,000 when he died childless in 1751; the Appleton farm passed to Thomas Case, a grandson of William Clayton.[26]

(d) Businessmen

The four businessmen, all absentees, who invested in land had 16% by value of the freehold land. Ralph Davenport, a merchant of Chorley, Lancs, had 312 acres worth £175 p.a. and was the largest landowner among the sixty-two freeholders. His grandfather bought at auction in 1728 and never lived in Crowley. Thomas Sutton, a bodice-maker of Crompton, Lancs, and Thomas Partington of Manchester, clockmaker, were also never residents. But Thomas Eaton's ancestors had lived for at least a century on the farm of seventy-four acres worth £41 p.a. in Crowley before he inherited it in 1728. Two of his father's sisters had married businessmen, one in Liverpool and the other in Northwich; and it may have been one of these uncles who encouraged him to go to sea as a teenager and become a merchant shipowner. He never returned to farm at Crowley and twenty-five years later he sold his land.

(e) Gentlemen and working farmers

We now come to the last and largest group of freeholders, the gentlemen and working farmers who jointly held 35% of the freehold land. Whereas most of the professionals, clergy and businessmen (with 33% altogether) and the gentry (with 25%) were not residents, the farmers were almost all living in the area. Perversely, the largest, Thomas Hough, with 177 acres in Crowley worth £99 p.a., was not, though he was a working farmer living at nearby Sutton Weaver. His family had been leaseholders in the Warburton manor of Sutton Weaver since at least 1572. Sutton is on the bank of the river Weaver where it enters the Mersey estuary; the main road from Chester to Warrington crossed the river by the old Frodsham Bridge and climbed the steep hill through Sutton Weaver. It is no great surprise to find that the Quakers, whose beliefs appealed so strongly to travelling merchants and tradespeople, had established a meeting in Sutton at this important trading junction before 1650 and that Thomas and Ellin Hough belonged to it when their eldest son, also called Thomas, was born in 1651. Our Thomas, born 1688, was one of the large family which the second Quaker Thomas and his wife Ellin had between 1677 and 1688.[27] His father had increased the family holding by taking two more leaseholds before 1700, and they added another in 1712, so that they were then farming a total of about 100 acres. Thomas invested his profits after 1730 in the purchase of freehold farms in Crowley, Antrobus and Over Whitley. By the time of his death in 1768, these amounted to some 270 acres with an annual value in excess of £150. With the failure of his three children to produce any heirs, this fortune was distributed around 1800 to dozens of cousins all over the north of England with occupations as various as combmaker, grocer, ironmonger, hingemaker, soap boiler, sailclothmaker and shipowner. There was even one with a sugar business in Demerara.[28]

Mrs Lydia Badley of Appleton Lower Town may have belonged to a more typical family of freehold farmers. Her father, Thomas Southern, farmed eighty-five acres (worth around £45 p.a. in 1744) at Bellfield and had at least fifty-seven acres more in Stretton which were let out to tenants. These had all been in his family since at least 1666, so he was quite a rich man. But he was illiterate; both he and his wife made their mark on their marriage settlement in 1695. He died in 1714 leaving Lydia an heiress at the age of thirteen. In 1725 she married John Bate, who soon inherited from his father the family's ancient tenement, Bate's Mill, Stockton Heath, with the water corn mill, the windmill and the malt kiln behind it, and also lands in Latchford and Lower Walton. Thomas Southern had bought a lease of the Warburton family's Old Warren (eighty-six acres) on the downs beside Bellfield (now the golf course) and John Bate had a lease of Stockton Heath House and another fifty acres, so he was probably farming over 250 acres and was the most prosperous resident in Appleton with an income of over £100 p.a. When he died unexpectedly in 1734/5 Lydia inherited all this for life under the terms of the marriage settlement, so it is not surprising that Mr Richard Badley had snapped up the rich widow by 1736. When she died in early 1750, her only daughter and heiress, Mary Bate, who was married to Nathan Caldwell, a grocer in Warrington, quickly arranged to sell all the Appleton lands to Sir Peter Warburton.[29]

Among the smaller freeholders in the 1740s were the Vernons of Gravestones, Aston. They had bought this farm of forty-eight acres (worth £30 p.a.) in 1659. The name was given to it in the nineteenth century when the graves of Jonathan and Sarah Vernon, who both died in 1692, were discovered there. They had two sons. The younger, Jonadab, was sent to learn the law with Richard Arderne of Stockport, though he seems later to have practised principally in Northwich. He was childless but evidently very successful in his profession. In his will of 1752 he left more than £2,500 to his nephews and nieces and their children and was able to ask for his coffin bearers to include George Eaton, esq., of The Pole, as well as Thomas Maddock, esq., late mayor of Chester, and Ralph Barrow, the principal salt merchant in Northwich.[30]

Jonadab's elder brother Jonathan inherited Gravestones and in 1698 he married Mary Lowe who had the rather large portion of £400, so their marriage settlement gave her the right to the property for life if she was left a widow. They lived and farmed there and had five sons of whom four were living when he died in 1728. The eldest, Jonathan, born in 1702, although entitled to the property on his mother's death under the marriage settlement, had already moved to Knutsford, where he was presumably apprenticed to some trade. There was a smaller property at Wincham which seems to have been sold about this time and the proceeds provided at least £100 for each of the three younger sons. John, the second son, stayed and worked the farm, presumably paying a rent to his mother, who moved to Knutsford, and the youngest, Ralph, became an apothecary in Knutsford.

Jonathan, in Knutsford, married Ann, who, giving no portion, got no marriage settlement, and they had a son and a daughter. When he fell ill in July 1734 he and his mother hurried to resettle the property on these children and provide an annuity of £5 p.a. for Ann if left a widow. He died in September and his young son six months later, leaving his only daughter, Mary, heiress of the farm on her grandmother's death. She was brought up by her mother, Ann, in Knutsford and when she inherited in 1753 mother and daughter settled accounts between themselves and it was agreed that Ann was owed £50 spent in bringing up Mary, £50 left by her husband's will, and her £5 p.a. annuity. She was not finally paid until 1764, on Mary's marriage to John Seddon of Knutsford. They sold the farm in 1777 for £1,750.[31] In this example we see not only the steady drift of these small freeholder families into the towns and the wealth the successful ones could make there, but also how widow Mary had an income of about £30 p.a. because of her marriage settlement, while widow Ann, without one, had only £5 p.a.

Another example which illustrates the same themes in a different arrangement is provided by the Pimlow family of Budworth. In 1716 William Pimlow I took a twenty-one-year lease of the Brownslow House Farm of eighty-nine acres in Great Budworth from Mary Bathurst of

Covent Garden, London. In February 1723 she sold it to him and Thomas Anderton of Hield, Aston, for £1,180 and in July 1724 they sold sixty-two acres of it for £1,231 to Thomas Partington of Manchester, whose son we met earlier as a clockmaker and owner of this farm in 1744. This clever bit of dealing gave the two families a profit of £50 and twenty-seven acres near Budworth Heath which William Pimlow I kept and added to the nine acres he had at Goldmine Farm. When he died in 1724 he put all his lands in trust to pay his widow Mary £8 p.a., to raise £500 for his six younger children and the balance for his eldest son William II. In 1738 William II, aged 30, married Ann Poole (born in Budworth in 1711), orphaned niece of Thomas Anderton of Hield, who gave £50 to add to the £70 she already possessed to make a portion of £120. All the lands were settled on their children and a £10 annuity was provided for Ann if left a widow. But William II survived only until April 1740 when he left Ann with a daughter, Mary, aged six months. She renewed the lease of 60/61 High Street with Sir George Warburton in June 1740 and raised a mortgage of £166 13s. 4d. from her brother or uncle, John, of Salisbury Court, Fleet Street, London, to pay the two youngest children of William Pimlow I the one-sixth each of £500 their father had left them. Before she was twenty-one Mary Pimlow, the heiress of this property, married Peter Penney of Knutsford, a thread merchant (one of the merchants who organized the flax spinning done by outworkers for which the Knutsford area was famous at this time). The property was resettled when she was 21 in 1761 and the new trustees were his brother Henry Penney, the best apothecary in Knutsford, and her uncles Thomas Poole, the principal plumber and glazier of Knutsford, and John Poole, coachmaker of Long Acre, London. Henry Penney advanced £300 on mortgage to his brother Peter, but unfortunately the latter went bankrupt in 1764. Because of the trust, enough was saved from this disaster to allow Peter and Mary Penney to bring up their children in Budworth, and their two sons appear again in the records in 1792 as Thomas of London, druggist (evidently the new word for apothecary), and Peter of Liverpool, gentleman. Again this illustrates the close connections between the landowners and the leading merchants and tradespeople of the towns.[32]

★　　★　　★

Table 2 (see p. 11) enumerates 132 leaseholders, but three of the four farmer-freeholders at whom we have looked also had leaseholds. This was commonplace. There was no dividing line. Among the large leaseholders in our sample, Samuel Glover leased 102 acres in Aston from the Leicesters and seventy-seven from the Warburtons. He had about ten acres freehold in Crowley and also about forty acres at the Reed House in Antrobus, just across the border from his Hollin Hall leasehold.[33] James Birchall had a freehold of fifty-five acres in Crowley but he and his wife preferred to live on the Aston leaseholds which they inherited from her family, probably cousins of the Vernons of Gravestones. He may indeed by this date have given the Crowley freehold to his daughter, who had married the Revd John Boardman, the third generation of his family to be rectors of Grappenhall.[34]

Leaseholds were a sort of half freehold, so the average leasehold farmer was less rich than his freehold neighbour. Robert Dewsbury of Aston is an example. His family had been on the twelve acres now known as the 'Old Shop' since at least 1572. Only four of the Aston leaseholders of 1749 had inherited from people of the same surname successively from before 1700, so to go back to 1572 was definitely unusual.[35] Before 1718 Robert Dewsbury, father of our Robert, bought his son the lease of East Feldy and forty-four acres. The father died about 1721 and the son farmed both properties and evidently became sufficiently prosperous to build himself a new house in 1731 and proud enough to put on it 'Robert and Hannah Dewsbury 1731' (Plate 4). They seem to have had about ten children between 1715 and 1730 but only five were still alive when he died in 1751. He left the 'Old Shop' to his son Samuel with the duty to pay £20 to his daughter Mrs Margaret Johnson of Mere, being the remainder of her portion; and he left East Feldy, where Samuel was farming, to his son John, who was charged with paying his debts and a sum of £60 to his unmarried daughter Martha as her portion. She was to provide with this money for her son 'Thomas Eaton otherwise Dewsbury now an infant' until he was fourteen. John had also to pay his mother £5 a year for her life. Robert, his third son, was, so to speak, cut off with one shilling, but whether this was because he had already had his portion or because he was out of favour is not known.[36]

The Dewsburys were not quite as well off as the Vernons and the

Pimlows but they were still comfortable, with an 'unearned' income of more than £30 p.a. between the two brothers. The very small leaseholders, those with only a cottage and a garden worth £1 10s. 0d. to £8 p.a., were significantly different, as two examples will make clear. Samuel Pickering, a carpenter/sawyer, was born in 1704. He and his wife Elizabeth, who was a year younger, had their first child in 1732 and six more by 1748. They paid £9 for the lease of the cottage in Aston in 1739 and the three lives

Plate 4: The Old Shop, Aston by Budworth, built in 1731 by Robert Dewsbury, a three-life leaseholder of fifty-six acres. The gabled wing on the right was added to the original house at the end of the nineteenth century.

were the two parents and their three-year-old son Samuel. The rent was 2s. 4d. a year and, judging from its size, as shown on the 1744 map, it had only one room. The son followed his father in the trade and they had several employees by 1750. A second leaseholder, Richard Hind, obtained a lease and built his cottage in 1708. Like all leaseholders he would have been given the timber by the estate, which owned all the trees on leasehold land. He seems to have spent all his life as a labourer around Aston. Born about 1680, he and his wife Rachel had eleven children between 1705 and

1726, all of whom apparently survived childhood. Most went away, but two or three stayed and one of these, Joseph, aged twenty-two, renewed the lease in 1741 using his own name and that of his sister Rachel, aged nineteen, as two of the 'lives'. Another brother, Isaac, fished Budworth Mere for the Warburtons and brought up a couple of children in Aston. The family had a net-making skill and, after 1750, regularly supplied nets to Arley for the garden and fishing. These two stories highlight one of the merits of this type of tenure, which brought the possibility of owning property within reach of the lower-paid workman. As we have seen, Sam Pickering was able to buy his lease for £9, less than half a year's wages. He actually charged himself out at 1s. 4d. a day (or £20 16s. 0d. a year). Perhaps the house had only one room, but it did make it possible for a hardworking and enterprising man to house himself and his wife for their lives and perhaps his son too.

IV

The Families Resident in Aston by Budworth, c. 1750

TABLE 6   *Families resident in Aston by Budworth, c. 1750*

1. Families farming more than 5 acres (*see also Table 7*)	
(a) Freeholders and three-life leaseholders	23
(b) Tenants paying rack rent	20
2. Poor (*see also Table 8*)	14
3. Families with other occupations (not poor) (*see also Table 9*)	21
Total	78

In the previous section we were looking at property-owners, here the focus, through Table 6, is on residents. Representative families of the freeholders and leaseholders – Sir Peter Warburton, the Vernons and the Dewsburys – have been described (and see Table 7). The most important of the tenant farmers were those farming on Arley demesne (see Map 2), who are listed in Appendix 2.12. The largest farm in the township, of 240 acres, known as Cowhouses, was at Arley Green and had been the sixteenth- and

TABLE 7 *Families resident in Aston farming more than five acres*

Freeholders including Sir P. Warburton (Appendix 2.1)	4
Warburton three-life leaseholders (Appendix 2.2)	16
Leicester and Daniel leaseholders (Appendix 2.3)	3
On Arley demesne (Appendix 2.12)	5
Tenants of the above categories:	
Freeholders	1
Warburton three-life leaseholders	4
Leicester and Daniel leaseholders	3
Other farmers in tithe list of 1752, farming 'let' land:	
Elias Berry, Ezekiel Eaton, Thomas Moore,	
Thomas Prescot, Jeffrey Rigby, Thomas Starkey,	
John Worsley	7

Total farmers 43

Notes:
1. Families having two or more holdings are only counted once.
2. All known members of one family are counted as one family, i.e. Peter Buckley and Ann Amery.
3. This list includes three farmers who were alive in 1749 and so appear in Appendices 2.2 and 2.3 but died before 1752 and so are not included in the tithe list for that year. But the 'foot and mouth' epidemic of 1750 had reduced the number of small farmers, so a total of 43 may be more correct for the late 1740s.

TABLE 8 *Poor in Aston by Budworth, 1753*

Every Christmas Sir Peter Warburton killed a bull and distributed the meat and 1s. per head to the poor. This is the earliest list to survive.

Name	No. in family (as per list)	Notes (not in original)	Symbol F = Family O = Old
Armstrong, Hugh	5	Thatcher with 4 children under 7.	F
Barker, Joseph	3	3 children 1740–45.	F
Barker, widow	3	Died 1756. Mary died 1757?	O
Barton, John	2	'lives in Budworth but belongs to Aston', born 1690s?	O
Berry, Jonathan	2	See leaseholders, Appendix 2.2; a sheep shearer.	
Chorton, Edward	6	Regular Arley labourer. 5 children under 10.	F
Cook, Samuel	4	See Leicester leaseholds, Appendix 2.3. 4 or 5 young children.	F
Eyes, Thomas, snr	1	Thatcher and paviour born 1680s? Had 4 children 1713–22; see his son under 'Other Families'.	

Hind, Richard	1	See leaseholders, Appendix 2.2. Born 1680, died 1768 aged 88.	O
Holland, Elizabeth	1		
Holland, Joseph	1		
Houghton, Isaac	4	See demesne tenants, Appendix 2.12. Born *c.* 1700. Labourer, had 6 children between 1728 and 1743. Had been a tenant farmer.	F
Hulme, Jonathan	2	Born 1690s?	O
Mann, widow	2	Probably widow of Edward Mann, carpenter, died 1723.	O
Millington, William	2	Born 1680s?	O
Moore, Peter	5		F
Moore, George	5	Regular Arley labourer. 4 children under 10.	F
Moore, John	3	Regular Arley labourer. 1 young child.	F
Moore, William	4	Regular Arley labourer. 2 small children.	F
Pickering, Peter	2	Shared cottage on Budworth Heath with W. Yarwood. A carrier – see text.	
Pickering, Samuel	4	See leaseholders. Had 7 children 1732–44 – see text.	F
Richardson, Richard	3	Miller, see leaseholders, Appendix 2.2.	F
Robinson, Charles	3		F
Robinson, Elizabeth	1		
Seddon, James	2	Related to Elizabeth Seddon, leaseholder?	
Spragg, widow	1	Widow of Thomas, see Daniel leaseholders, Appendix 2.3, died 1753.	O
Toft, Edward	5	Regular Arley labourer. 3 young children.	F
Winstanley, widow	2	Related to the two boys Mark and Thomas who worked for Arley.	O
Walton, John	6	Part-time labourer living in Crowley with 3 young children.	F
Yarwood, William	2	See Budworth leaseholders, Appendix 2.5. Arley labourer.	

Notes:
1. The dates of births and deaths and children are from parish registers but identifications are always uncertain.
2. Where, as with Hugh Armstrong, the 'number in family' seems inconsistent with the number of children, I do not know whether there is an unrecorded death or whether working husbands did not count.
3. Totals: 30 household heads; 87 individuals; 6 women; 24 men; *c.* 14 working men with children. The remainder were probably too old, too ill or too crippled to earn a reasonable living.

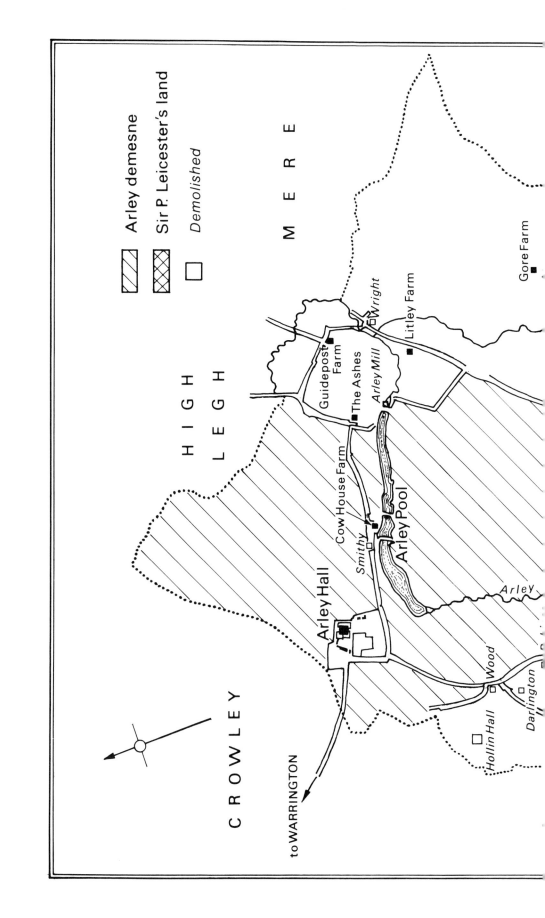

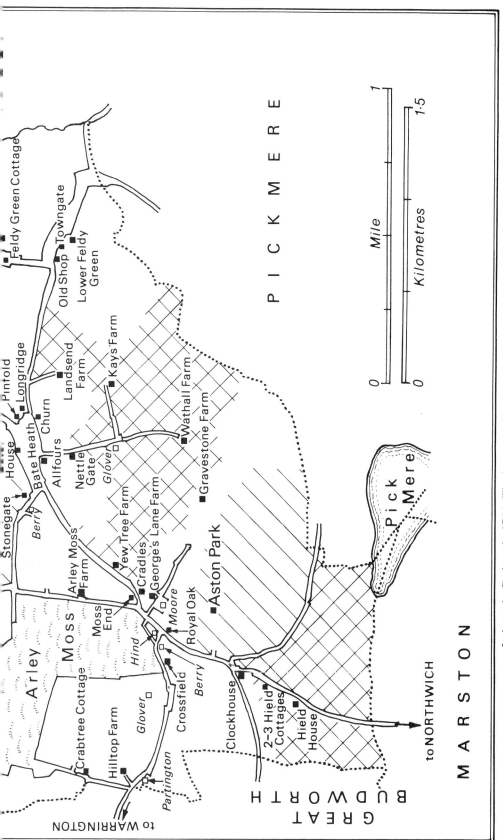

2. Aston by Budworth, 1744. The lanes, the Heaths, the Greens and Arley Moss formed the commons on which property owners were entitled to graze their animals. The roads were not paved at this period except for a narrow 'causey' for pedestrians and horses.

seventeenth-century home farm. Thomas Birchall, who leased this farm and Arley Mill, and Samuel Dutton, who had 192 acres at The Gore, were substantial commercial farmers who each had several hundred pounds of working capital invested and expected to make good profits in excess of their large rack rents. They were probably related to the property-owning Birchalls of Appleton and Duttons of Great Budworth. The latter's son-in-law Thomas Hewitt (listed in Table 9) was possibly managing The Gore for his father-in-law between 1743 and 1753. Whether he was paid more by his father-in-law than the £50 a year Sir Peter Warburton paid him in 1754–7 for managing the Arley estate we do not know. Both these farms and the 114 acres that the Hon. John Smith Barry had at Aston Park would have needed to employ labourers. In addition to these three large farms, which included the only three houses on the demesne, there were five three-life leaseholders who were renting additional acres to improve the size of their farms, and two farmers with houses in High Legh and Crowley doing the same. Ralph Kinsey rented sixty-eight acres of demesne to add to the seven acres beside Ruth Tovey's cottage, where he was probably living.

Several of the tenants who were renting their farms from the freeholders and three-life leaseholders had quite large farms. Ottiwell Broom managed the 135 acres at Litley with the assistance of his wife and seven children, of whom four were apparently adults when he died in 1753, so he probably did not employ farm labour.[37] The smallest tenants, to judge from the tithe lists of 1752 and 1753[38] showing some with only an acre or two of arable and two or three cows, were barely full-time farmers and may have been supplementing their incomes by doing carting or ditching on contract for the larger farmers. It was such people, whose farming capital was perhaps only £20 and who were earning from their farming venture only slightly more than they could have earned as labourers, who were most at risk from an unexpected disaster like the cattle plague (probably foot and mouth disease), which could force them back to being labourers.

The list of poor families (Table 8) who were given a Christmas present of meat and money by the Warburtons in 1753 can be divided into three groups: eight too old to earn enough; fourteen with children; and eight others. Of the families with children, seven fathers appear regularly as labourers on the Arley home farm in the estate accounts. Two others, the thatcher Hugh Armstrong and Sam Pickering the carpenter/sawyer, worked frequently for the Warburtons charging themselves out at 1s. 4d. a

TABLE 9 *Families in Aston with other occupations – not poor*

1. FAMILIES WITH LEASES TO PROPERTY

Name	See Appendix	Notes
Berry, Charles	2.2	Arley labouring family?
Beswick, William	2.12	Blacksmith at Arley Green
Cooke, John	2.3	Unknown
Hind, Joseph	2.2	See text for description of family
Richardson, Richard	2.3	Old clockmaker
Seddon, Elisabeth	2.2	Old widow?
Tovey, Ruth	2.3	Old widow

2. FAMILIES LIVING AS SUB-TENANTS

These are all fathers whose names appear in the parish register as resident in Aston at the birth of a child 1742-1750 and who were not property owners, tenants, farmers or poor as listed in Tables 7, 8, and 9.

Name	Notes
Banner, Holford	Doctor of Medicine. In Aston 1747–50. In Budworth 1753.
Barker, John	Had 4 children 1738–46. Possibly died 1750.
Bushell, Matthew	Clockmaker. Moved to Clockhouse (named after his occupation) in 1754.
Eyes, Thomas	Thatcher and paviour. Son of old man of same name. See table 8.
Hewitt, Thomas	Married Elizabeth, daughter of Samuel Dutton of the Gore Farm, where he probably helped his father-in-law while they had 5 children 1743–53. He was steward of the Arley estate 1754–57.
Hind, Isaac	Fisherman of Budworth Mere, living with father. See table 8.
Holland, Benjamin	Child 1741. Regular Arley labourer 1751.
Holt, George	Children 1750–51. Assistant to Sam Pickering at 1s. per day.
Hough, John	Child 1751.
Johnson, John	Child 1747.
Lee, John	Tailor, 3 children 1743–45. Possibly died 1748.
Mann, Caleb and John	Children 1744 and 1746, probably sons of E. Mann carpenter. (see table 8 for his widow). They may have been carpenters.
Robinson, John	Regular Arley labourer 1751. But were the children born 1743–49 his or those of his namesake the leaseholder?

Notes:
1. There are a large number of uncertainties involved in converting the names in Tables 8 and 9 into thirty-five 'families'. This number must be regarded as very approximate.

day, but had large families to support. Richard Richardson probably operated Arley Mill but nothing is known of the other four. Among the group of eight others, William Yarwood worked as a labourer in the gardens at Arley and Peter Pickering, who lived with him (both had wives) in the cottage on Budworth heath, was a carrier who operated between Budworth and Chester.[39] Two others, Seddon and Winstanley, were probably related to people who worked at Arley. On the other four single people I have no information. Among those whose occupations are unknown some are very likely to have been working on the large farms mentioned earlier and some were probably too ill or crippled to earn a living. The poor rate raised £46 in Aston in 1750 but there is no record of its distribution.

Among the families listed in Table 9 we can identify two professional and managerial men. One, a young doctor, Holford Banner, the son of a Cheshire doctor, had recently arrived in Aston and was to spend his life in Great Budworth; the other, Thomas Hewitt, we have already noted as manager of the Arley estate 1754–7. There were two clockmakers, one old and one young, possibly apprenticed earlier to the other. The other craftsmen include a blacksmith, a thatcher and paviour, a fisherman and a net-maker, a tailor, and at least one carpenter. Three families are labourers but they are not 'poor' because they are the type who were on the verge of being tenant farmers or agricultural contractors. Ben Holland had certainly been a tenant farmer a few years earlier.

These are the seventy-eight families counted in Aston. On a conventional demographer's view of 4.75 persons to a family this suggests 370 persons (78 × 4.75) in 1750 compared with 396 enumerated in the 1801 census. Clearly we are in the right area but there are too many uncertainties to hope for numerical accuracy. One important clarification is required. It was an old country custom for young people to move from their parents' house and live and work on another farmer's land. John Holland tells us in his evidence on the Arley Moss enclosure[40] that he went to work at Hield in 1742 aged ten and stayed there until he was nineteen. A very important part of the agricultural labour force comprised young men and women (women always had charge of the dairy and cheesemaking in Cheshire) between the ages of ten and thirty. If a farmer had too many or too few children, he could balance his labour force through these living-in young, unmarried workers. Although servants, they were regarded as part of the family. The only direct evidence we have on servants in 1750 is those at Arley Hall, where Table 10 shows there were sixteen, all unmarried and living and eating in the house.[41] There were six people in the Warburton household at this time, two young children, a grandmother and an old cousin as well as Sir Peter and Lady Elizabeth. So the cooks and maids were looking after twenty-two people including themselves. One of the day labourers, married and living out, helped carry fuel, water, etc. about the

TABLE 10 *Servants at Arley Hall, 1750*

	Salary £
Sir Peter's man	15
Lady Elizabeth's maid	5
Lady Elizabeth's footman	6
A cook	6
Undercook	3
Three maids	3 each
A coachman	10
Groom (adult)	6
Postillion (youth)	3
Carter/foreman of the farm	6
Dairymaid	3
Gardener (skilled)	8
Gamekeeper	7
Accountant/Manager	20

TABLE 11 *Housing in Aston by Budworth, 1744*

	Number of houses[42]
On Arley estate, including the Hall shown on 1744 map	43
On Leicester lands	9
On Daniel land	2
Other freeholders, including house and cottage at Litley	5
Total	59

house and two more regularly worked in the gardens (see Table 8). If this was the position for a man of Sir Peter's income, it seems likely that most farms only had a boy who assisted on the farm and carried fuel, etc., and a girl who helped the farmer's wife in the dairy, garden and kitchen, and in the summer with the harvest.

Now let us look at housing. Table 11 identifies fifty-nine houses in Aston by Budworth (Plate 5). We have seen earlier that Richard Rutter, esq., provided two rooms in a farmhouse for his widow and it is a common feature of other property-owners' wills to leave the use of a room and the oven for a widow's life. So we know that house-sharing was common among the richer groups. William Stout[43] rented his room and his board in different houses on one occasion and he shared a house at another time. The overseers of the poor of Sevenoaks (another township in Great Budworth parish) put three or even four families in one house in 1758.[44] We must therefore assume it is correct that our seventy-eight families

Plate 5: Towngate, Aston by Budworth. Most houses were like this in the 1740s – timber-framed, single-storey, with a thatched roof. (The porch is modern.) Brick houses as in Plates 2, 3 and 4 were still rare in this area.

squeezed themselves, complete with their old grandparents, etc., into fifty-nine houses.

This, then, is the picture of Aston. It was a place where farming was what life was about, like hundreds of other townships in England. What made it different was having Arley Hall, with 1,200 acres of demesne land, in its midst. Apart from the building itself, at this time a great crumbling half-timbered palace with a 115-ft frontage of three storeys, the big difference it made to the community was to bring fifteen or twenty families to serve its needs. They were mostly labourers to work the land but there were a few craftsmen to look after the house and its barns, stables and gardens. The Warburtons were much less powerful in township affairs than they were to become a century later, when every other resident was a tenant. In 1750 there were another gentleman, three freeholders and twenty leaseholders – all men of property. Apart from the seven houses on Arley demesne all the other 52 houses had been built and were effectively owned and maintained by others.

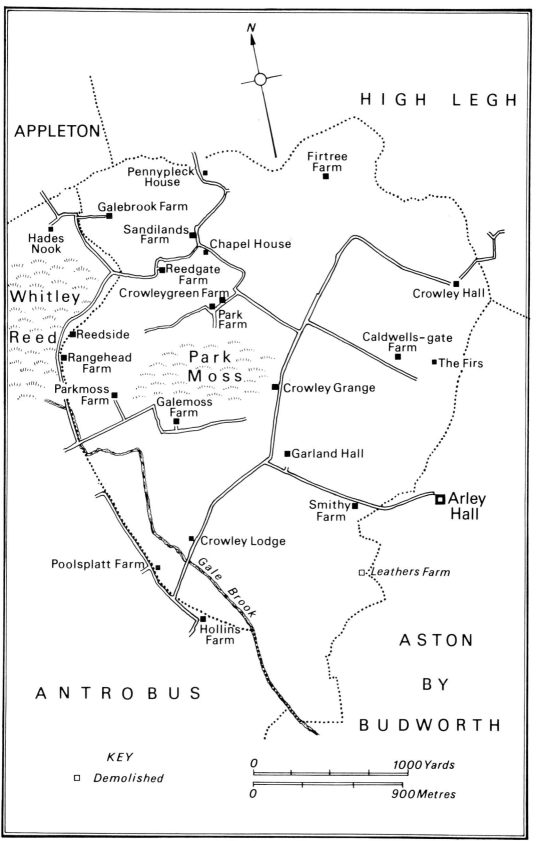

N

HIGH LEGH

APPLETON

Pennypleck House

Firtree Farm

Galebrook Farm

Sandilands Farm

Hades Nook

Chapel House

Whitley

Reedgate Farm

Crowleygreen Farm

Crowley Hall

Reed

Park Farm

Reedside

Caldwells-gate Farm

Rangehead Farm

Park Moss

The Firs

Parkmoss Farm

Crowley Grange

Galemoss Farm

Garland Hall

Arley Hall

Smithy Farm

Crowley Lodge

Poolsplatt Farm

Gale Brook

Leathers Farm

Hollins Farm

ASTON

BY

ANTROBUS

BUDWORTH

KEY

□ Demolished

0   1000 Yards

0   900 Metres

3. Crowley, *c.* 1750.

V

The Three Other Townships Described

(a) Crowley

Although Crowley was so close to Arley Hall (see Map 3), in 1750 the Warburtons did not own a square yard there. It was wholly in the hands of seventeen freeholders, who, with one exception, let their lands in 1750 to tenants at rack rents. I have been able to trace only two or three families of resident labourers, so living-in servants or people from Budworth must have fulfilled their labour requirements. A century earlier during the Civil War there may have been thirty or forty owner-occupied farms there but as they were sold they were consolidated into fewer units at the same time as investors were replacing working farmers as the owners. Table 12 shows the approximate number of farms in owner-occupation in Crowley by decades from 1690 to 1760. This signals quite a social revolution. We have

TABLE 12 *Number of owner-occupied farms in Crowley, 1690–1760* [45]

1690	1700	1710	1720	1730	1740	1750	1760
15	12	12	11	8	2–4	1–2	1

seen earlier that 25% of the freehold land in the four townships was owned by gentry who were not owner-occupiers and 33% by businessmen, churchmen and other professionals who were purely investors, but that this left 35% in the hands of the farming people. Table 6 showed that twenty-three of the forty-three farmers in Aston were freeholders or leaseholders.[46] Why was the proportion so much less in Crowley?

I think the answer is that Crowley was isolated: there was no main road, no church (although possibly a chapel) and no alehouse or inn. As the number of freeholders in the area declined it became steadily less attractive for those who remained. It confirms this view that James Birchall preferred his leasehold house at Moss End, Aston, to his Crowley freehold.

(b) Appleton

The Higher Town of Appleton was, like Crowley and Aston, a community of farmers, but it had a character of its own. The heart of the area was the

38

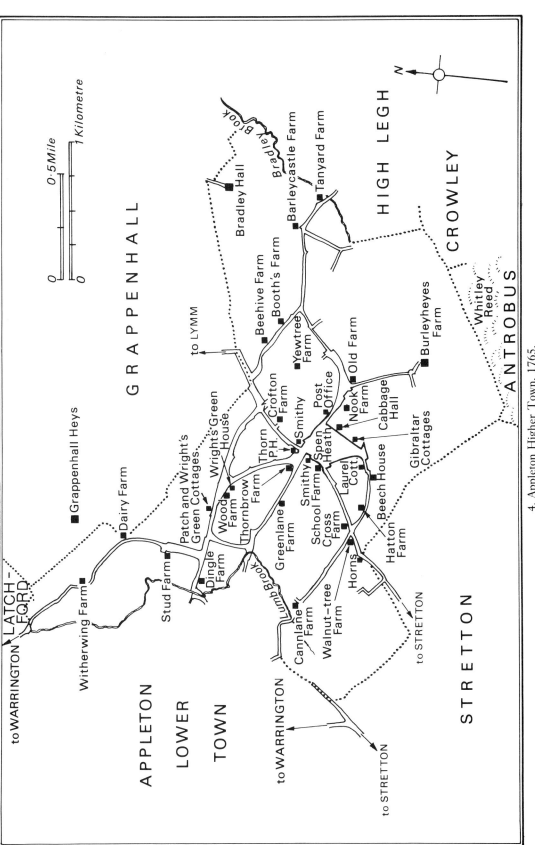

4. Appleton Higher Town, 1765.

Spen Heath common, through which ran the road along the ridge from Chester via Stretton to High Legh and Lymm (see Map 4). At the junction with the road to Warrington was the Thorn public house with a blacksmith's shop opposite it on both roads. A string of buildings along Pepper Street and Hatton's windmill completed the circle of the common. It evidently made a sufficiently attractive place to have retained the affections of a number of the leaseholders who continued to live and farm there. Unfortunately, much less evidence survives about Appleton than about the other three townships: no tithe returns identify the farmers, there are no lists of the poor, and large numbers of the baptisms and burials by this period were registered at other churches – Grappenhall or Daresbury, both much closer than Great Budworth, and the Baptist chapel. But two old leaseholder families still lived there. The Caldwells and the Clares had held Warburton lands since the middle of the sixteenth century. In 1744 Joseph Caldwell was at Beehive Farm and John was the host at the Thorn and his farm buildings were at what is now called Thornbrow Farm. The Clares had been at Burleyheyes since at least the last decade of the seventeenth century and Thomas, who died in 1724, had been so successful that he was able to leave more than £1,250 in cash to his children as well as leasehold lands in High Legh and Burleyheyes itself.[47]

Appleton Lower Town was a much more commercial place (see Map 5). The main road south from Scotland through Lancashire crossed the Mersey by the Warrington Bridge – the only bridge over the Mersey west of Manchester. It then ran on a long causeway beside the Mersey to Wilderspool, where the road to Chester went off westwards and the London Road – still so called – went straight on over Stockton Heath and up the long hill through Appleton to Stretton. As one might expect there is some evidence for a trading bustle at Wilderspool, beside the Mersey, where the Saracen's Head Inn stood.[48] It is a pity we know so little about it. A short way nearer London on the north edge of Stockton Heath was a blacksmith's shop and no doubt more inns and other facilities for traders. On the eastern corner of the Heath was Bate's watermill, windmill and malt kiln. What had in the seventeenth century been a tract of poor hilly land was beginning to come alive with commercial activity. Land values were rising quite sharply, partly because the population of Warrington was getting larger and richer and therefore providing a better market for milk, butter, cheese and even grain. They were also rising because high lands commanding fine views over the Mersey estuary were becoming attractive

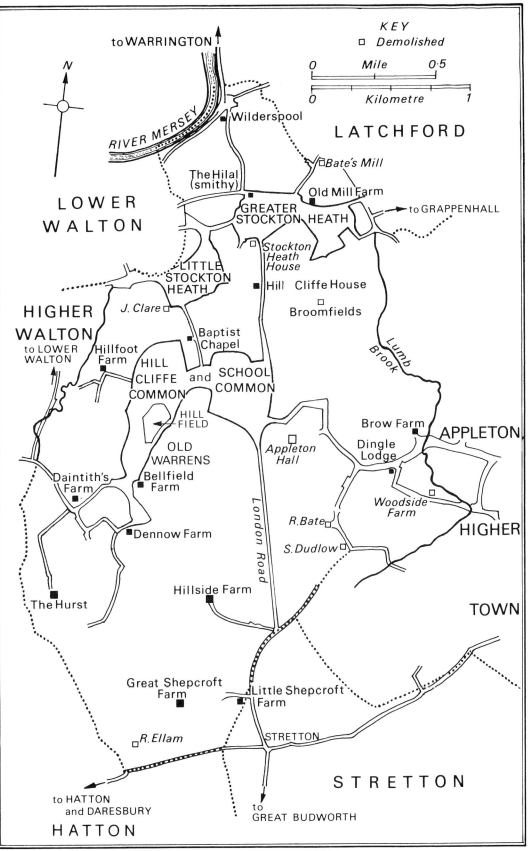

5. Appleton Lower Town, 1765.

for a new social phenomenon – gentlemen's houses. Two rich naval officers were to settle there in the 1750s and they were soon joined by rich businessmen escaping the growing smokiness of industrial life in Warrington and St Helens.

(c) Great Budworth

J. Aikin in his *Tour around Manchester*, 1795, noted that the character of Knutsford owed much to the large number of gentlemen's seats nearby. In a smaller way Great Budworth was the same (see Maps 6 and 7). Arley Hall, Aston Park, and The Pole have already been described. Marbury Hall, which looked at the town across Budworth Mere – or, as they called it, Marbury Mere – was inhabited from the late 1740s by the Hon. Richard Barry, younger son of the Earl of Barrymore, whose family had bought it from the Marburys at the beginning of the century. His younger brother John, we noted earlier, was in 1749 starting to build Belmont after pulling down the old Brownslane House, where his cousins Thomas and Elizabeth Yates had lived in the 1730s and early 1740s. In Comberbach lived Capt. James Pigott, who was related to the Leicesters at Tabley, and a number of successful Liverpool merchants.

These gentry went to church in Budworth and the maintenance of their large houses and expensive way of life helped to determine the type of tradespeople who lived there; services were also provided for a substantial group of professional people. The vicar from 1741 to 1787 was Richard Selby, who married Dorothy, sister of George Eaton of The Pole, and the two of them dominated affairs by attending every vestry meeting for forty years.[49] Although he had no church, the Rev. Simon Mills lived next to the George and Dragon in the 1750s and 1760s.[50] Beside the church in Budworth still stands the solid schoolhouse built in Elizabethan times. It had an endowment which provided a salary for the schoolmaster who was appointed, under the trust, by the vicar. Samuel Edwards was schoolmaster and parish clerk until his death in 1745. Although his wife Alice (née Brereton) owned property in Malpas and Denbighshire, she lived on in Budworth until she died in 1759.[51] He was followed by Ralph Briscall of Cogshall, who was schoolmaster in 1750, at which date the old school rooms were repaired by the churchwardens.[52] We have seen that Hamlet Yate retired to the Old Hall when he ceased to run the Arley estate and had to leave Aston Park. After he died in 1750 his unmarried daughter Mary

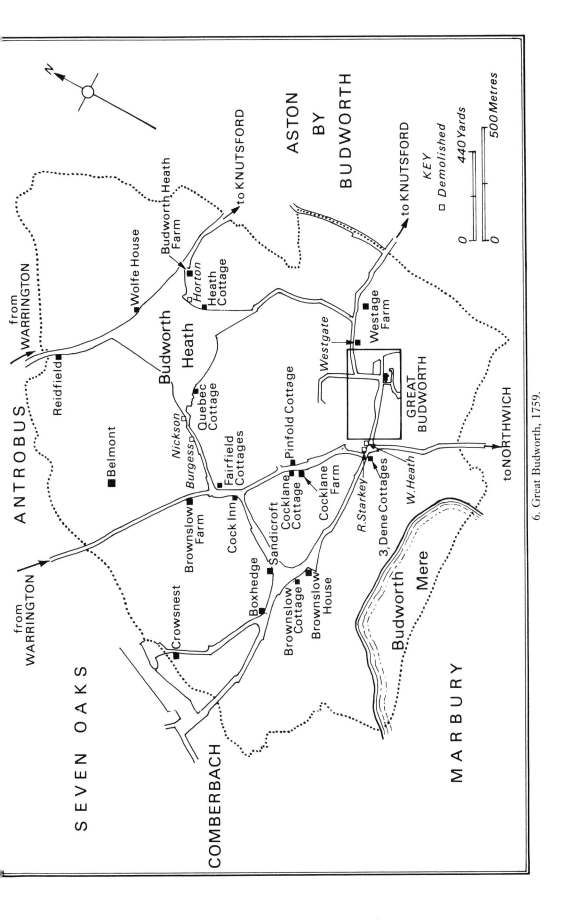

6. Great Budworth, 1759.

continued there until 1768, when Dr Holford Banner took over the house. Mr Peter Penney, husband of Mary Pimlow, retired to Budworth after his bankruptcy. Samuel Glover, the largest leaseholder in Aston, lived in the Henshall family's house from 1740 until he died in 1751 and his widow lived in the town for another 20 years. The other prosperous freeholders and leaseholders of Aston – James Birchall, the Vernons, the Forests and the Manns, the Duttons and Tofts of Wethale and Thomas Anderton of Hield – all used Budworth as their centre, as did the freeholders of Comberbach.

All these people gave character to the place, but the main reason for the development of Budworth as a town from the Middle Ages was the London road (now the A559). Great Budworth was a convenient stop for horse traffic some eight miles from Warrington. The Cock Inn on the main road was already flourishing in the seventeenth century and there is evidence for the existence of at least two more inns. One was run by the Heath family: the two Johns who died in 1739 and 1755 and the Samuel who died in 1738 all seem to have been involved, together with the Samuel who succeeded John as sexton in 1755 and the John who had a malt kiln in the 1760s. Another was run by Samuel Eaton, described as innkeeper in his will of 1758. Also, Thomas Dutton had licences as an alehouse keeper for several years in the 1740s and 1750s.[53] Perhaps the clearest evidence that Budworth was a place of local importance between 1730 and 1770 was the fact that the Officers of Excise (on ales and beers) were stationed in the town. These were officials of substance with a salary of about £50 a year and a complex system of allowances. The total numbers of baptisms and burials for Budworth township in the period 1727–55 is similar to the numbers for Aston by Budworth, so it is likely the two townships had a similar-sized population. The 1801 census counted 463 people in Budworth to 396 in Aston. But whereas Aston had 3,000 acres, Budworth only had 900, so it is likely that at least two-thirds of the Budworth population was not engaged in agriculture.

On the 1759 map of the Warburton family's land in Budworth are shown some fifty-six houses. The Leicester tenants had another twelve and the freeholders six, so there were about seventy-four houses in the town. Only about thirty freeholder and leaseholder families lived in Budworth, so all the rest of the population must have been tenants. Some of the richest of the freeholder/leaseholders, such as the Cooks, the Duttons and Alice Burgess, owned several houses and acted as landlords, letting out their

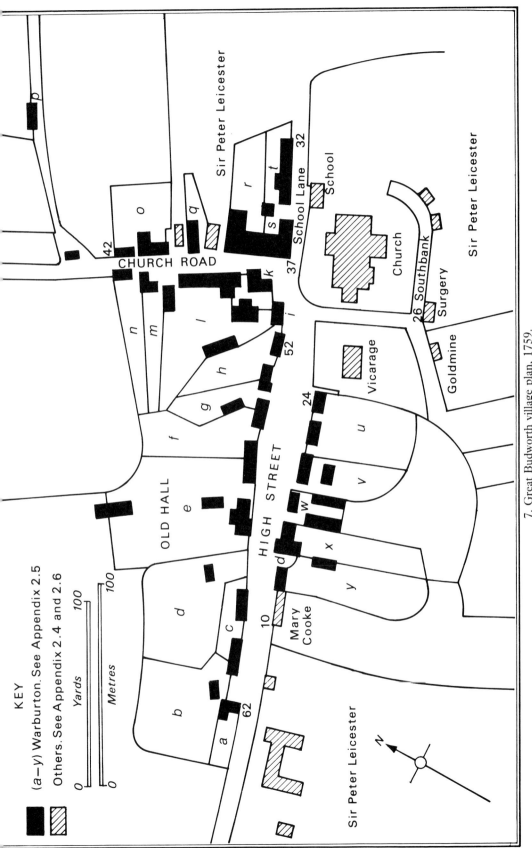

7. Great Budworth village plan, 1759.

KEY

(a–y) Warburton. See Appendix 2.5

Others. See Appendix 2.4 and 2.6

Yards
0   100
Metres
0   100

CHURCH ROAD

School Lane

Sir Peter Leicester

Sir Peter Leicester

Sir Peter Leicester

Sir Peter Leicester

OLD HALL

HIGH STREET

Mary Cooke

School

Church

Southbank Surgery

Goldmine

Vicarage

N

houses or rooms in them. Others, among the cottagers, were poor. When John Litler, carpenter, renewed the lease of 62 High Street, where his brother-in-law Samuel Fryar lived in 1739, he only paid £3 10s. 0d. to add two lives. If that represented five times the annual value, the cottage was only worth 14s. a year or £17 10s. 0d. freehold – eighteen months' wages for a labourer. It would have been a simple place indeed.

But what did the inhabitants all do? There is a great shortage of information. There may have been a few shops; Mr Deacon, a mercer who lived in Comberbach, may have had one. It was apparently the practice to expose goods for sale on Sundays after the morning service (a street market, perhaps) but some over-eager vendors had to be censured by the manor court for selling during the service. There was a fair three times a year, on 2 February, 25 March and 21 September, for horses, cattle and general merchandise. A detailed record of purchases in 1737/8 describes the horses bought or exchanged and gives details of the buyers and sellers and those who vouched for them. Clearly, fraud and theft were taken as serious risks. Only three horses were exchanged at each fair, so the institution was clearly not flourishing. But it survived into the 1750s and Sir Peter tried to stimulate business by having it 'cried' in the neighbouring towns. We know that there were at least three blacksmiths' shops and that among the leaseholders were two gardeners, two tailors, two carpenters and a chairmaker. Among the tenants was a builder, with no doubt a good number of building craftsmen of all kinds. There might have been people who worked with the blacksmiths, the saddlers and the wheelwrights. There were at least three carriers with horses and carts. There were surely lots of ostlers, stable hands and jolly buxom maids at the inns!

Such, then, is the picture of Great Budworth in the middle of the eighteenth century. It was not to last for long. Between 1753 and 1773 a new turnpike road was built from the London road at Cranage Green, north of Holmes Chapel, to Knutsford and on to Mere, where it divided, one branch going on through Altrincham to Manchester and the other westward to Warrington. This diverted the traffic away from the old road, which was clearly a lesser route when Burdett published the first really good map of Cheshire in 1777. The road became just the way from Warrington to Northwich and by the early nineteenth century Budworth was more a village than a town.

VI

Conclusions

This study of Great Budworth, Aston, Appleton and Crowley has aimed to describe the people who lived in the four townships in the 1740s, their occupations and incomes. It has revealed that each township had its own distinct character and thus cautions against overarching generalization. Although it is a snapshot of society in this decade, some information has been given about how people came to their position in the 1740s. This final section will describe the long-term trends that seem to emerge.

It has been mentioned on several occasions that property-owners of the 1740s possessed what had earlier been two or three separate farms. The notes in Appendix 2.11 on Crowley freeholders show that there had been at least thirty-four owners compared with the seventeen existing in 1749 and all the other tables in Appendix 2 show owners with more than one farm or house. So it is clear that in the fifty or 100 years before 1740 the number of farms and owners had been considerably reduced. It is also evident that in the 1740s many owners were no longer farming their lands. There was only one owner out of seventeen farming in Crowley, while there were twenty-three owner-farmers out of forty-three owners in Aston, and perhaps as many as half the farmers in Budworth were members of the families of the owners. The only evidence in this study for the number of owners who had farmed their own land earlier is for Crowley, where it has been found that nearly half the owners were still farming their own land in the 1690s. If this pattern of behaviour was true in the other townships and for leaseholders as well as freeholders – and there are many little indications in the tables and elsewhere that it was – then two other phenomena deserve attention: there must have been a large increase in the fifty years before 1740 in the number of tenant farmers paying a full rack rent and having only a lease for a period of years; and individual farms had increased considerably in size in these fifty years. Not much has been said in this study about tenant farmers[54] but a few general observations can be made. As they were not property-owners they had no capital invested in land and so people with less capital than the old freeholder/leaseholders were enabled to engage in the business of farming. We have seen that it was the custom for young men and women to live and work on other people's farms from the age of ten and that they received an annual wage which would have risen to about £6 p.a. for men at, say, twenty-one, £3 for women. If they saved this for several years – and there is evidence in these papers that some did – they would accumulate enough to have the working capital for a small farm. If either his or her family could give them a portion they might be able to marry and take a larger farm. One result, therefore, of the change to rack-rent tenancies was to open the risky business of farming to people lower down the income range. Indeed, every young labourer became a potential farmer.

It was observed when we were looking at the population of Aston that there were some fifteen or twenty families of labourers who seemed to be associated with the large farms which were mostly on the demesne. In Crowley there were only three families of labourers because there was no demesne and fewer large farms. So it seems likely that the movement towards larger farms was accompanied by an increase in the number of families of labourers. So it could be that the general movement was from a society in the middle of the seventeenth century with a large number of small farms occupied and run by their owners without the assistance of labourers (except living-in young people) towards one at the end of the eighteenth century with fewer but larger farms run by less well-capitalized rack-rented tenants employing growing numbers of families of labourers. This may partly explain the well-known and relentless rise of the poor rates (Table 13) and the appearance of a rural proletariat.

TABLE 13 *Poor rates (pence in the £ of annual value)*[55]

	1750	*1767–8 average*
Aston	7	21
Great Budworth	8	24
Appleton	14 (1749)	21

In our sample the freeholders and leaseholders emerge with 60% of the land by capital value compared with the 40% held by Sir Peter Warburton and the other large estate-owners. It would appear that the freeholder/leaseholder group of owners had been at least as important a century earlier and that although much of the land had changed hands in the fifty years before 1750[56] the large estate-owners in this sample had not increased their holdings significantly in this period. A process can be observed, of which examples have been given earlier, in which freeholder/ leaseholder families provided portions for their younger children. To do this they normally had to sell land or raise a mortgage. The majority of younger sons spent their portions being apprenticed to a trade (or the law) in the towns and in setting up in business, while daughters frequently took businessmen for husbands, so part of the agrarian capital went into trade. If the eldest son disdained the land he often raised a mortgage to set himself up and sold the farm only when he was well established. When land was sold the buyer was often someone who had made money in the towns and was looking for a safe investment.

These papers do not tell us why trade was so attractive, but William Stout has left us a first-hand account in his autobiography.[57] The younger son of a small freeholder near Lancaster, he was apprenticed and set up on his own as an ironmonger in Lancaster in 1688. Starting with a capital of £119 and borrowing a further £22, he made a clear profit of £50 his first year and averaged over £100 a year profit in the 1690s. There is nothing in his story to suggest he made innovations or was particularly clever. He was honest, capable and hardworking and lived a plain but comfortable life in the course of which he amassed more than £5,000. It is not surprising that he was often asked to take his relations' children into business. Nor should it be surprising that in almost every example of a freeholder/leaseholder that has been given earlier, some members of the family had been in trade (Plate 1). It would seem that the middling sort of landed property-owners in this area slowly moved themselves and their money into trade from the second half of the seventeenth century onwards. As the pace of commercial and industrial development accelerated after 1750 so their requirements for capital to finance the new activities increased. Their sales of land became more frequent, as details in the tables in Appendix 2 attest, and at the same time the commercial investors among them were inclined to move their capital back into trade. This social group provided many of the entrepreneurs of the industrial revolution in the Mersey basin, as well as an important part of the capital. Their departure from the land may have also provided an opportunity for the great old estates to purchase land and so to improve and reform the whole tangled and anomalous skein of landholding that had been inherited from the Middle Ages.[58] From these developments emerged the nineteenth-century situation, which was referred to earlier, in which almost all the land in the sample area was owned by the Warburtons, the Lyon and Parr families, bankers of Warrington, the Leigh family, salt merchants of Liverpool, and the Leicester family, who still held the 350 acres in Aston that they had acquired in the thirteenth century.

Appendices

APPENDIX 1 *Annual Values and the Land Tax*

1. *The land tax*

When the land tax was first levied in the mid-1690s there was no list of the value of every property in the country. It was therefore decided by parliament that every county and borough should have a quota fixed in money. County officials then divided these into quotas for every township or parish. Aston by Budworth, for example, was given a quota of £131 11s. 0d. when the rate of the land tax was at 4s. in the pound. If the rate for the year was fixed by parliament at 2s. in the pound then Aston would have to raise only £65 15s. 6d. These money quotas were never changed between 1697 and the end of the land tax in the nineteenth century.

The townships divided their quotas among their citizens by making a list of the annual rental value of all property in land and in money in the township, and dividing the quota in proportion to the annual value. As the quotas had been allocated without a knowledge of the annual values, the rate of the tax on the actual annual values varied between every township. Stories circulating in the early eighteenth century suggested that when the nominal rate was 4s. in the pound, actual rates of 3s. and 4s. were common in the south of England but that in the north actual rates were often only 1s. or 2s. in the pound. Where lists of these annual values have survived the problem for historians is to assess how close the listed values were to the actual rents being paid at the date of the list.[59]

2. *The surviving documents and their interpretation*

In the Warburton Muniment Box 25 Folder 1 are tax assessments and in Folder 2 are valuations. Both are grouped by manors.

Aston by Budworth

There is a Land Tax Duplicate which shows the annual value of each property and the tax assessed on it for 1741 in the form:

£70 0s. 0d. Sam Dutton for the Gore £5 12s. 0d.

Appendices 2.1, 2.2 and 2.3 reproduce these values, which I have attached to the correct properties based on rentals of 1749, other rentals, maps and their reference books, manor court call books, deeds and leases. The 1741 list omits the annual value of Arley Hall demesne lands (Appendix 2.12) but gives the tax payable as £44 16s. 0d. The remainder of Aston is valued at £1,103 7s. 0d. p.a. and the tax payable is £86 15s. 0d., which is 7.862%. Applying this percentage to £44 16s. 0d. gives an annual value to Arley demesne of £570. On the 1741 document a list has been added entitled 'Valuation of Arley Hall Demesne' which lists fifteen tenants and their rack rents totalling £427 12s. 6d., including several which are the same as in Appendix 2.12. The 'lands in hand' are valued at only £55. In Appendix 2.12 I have put a value of £215 on the 393 acres which Sir Peter was occupying round the Hall in 1749, which at just over 10s. an acre is more in line with the rest of the Aston values and makes the total value of the demesne lands £570 (S. Dutton for The Gore, which is valued separately in the 1741 return at £70, is included in Appendix 2.12 and makes the total value there £640). Most of the 4s. in the pound land tax charges were about 1s. 6d. in the pound on the annual values, but they vary a little. These discrepancies were probably caused by the adjustments made when farms were merged or divided and houses demolished or built.

The annual value given for Sam Dutton of £70 contrasts with his rent of £55 0s. 0d. and this is the only farm listed in Appendix 2.12 where the rack rent is not the same as the annual value. From the accounts for 1732–45 in Box 19 we can infer that he was granted a lease in 1733 by Thomas Slaughter, who had just taken over the management of the estate. In a case stated for counsel's advice in 1745 in Folder 10, Box 24, we learn that Sam Dutton was a friend of Thomas Slaughter and valued Aston Park at £70 so that Slaughter could get a lease from old Sir George Warburton at £70 p.a. and then let the property to others at £85. We are also told that Aston Park was such a good house that a gentleman would pay at least £100 p.a. for it. It appears that Sam Dutton and Thomas Slaughter had conspired to cheat

Sir George, because in 1748 Sir Peter let Aston Park to the Earl of Barrymore for £100 p.a. In 1754, when Dutton's twenty-one-year lease expired, he let The Gore at £80 a year.

From this analysis it can be seen that the annual value attributed to the Arley demesne lands is similar to the rack-rent value and as this annual value is on the same basis as the rest of Aston all these annual values must be similar to rack-rent values. This is confirmed by J. Brown's leasehold, which had an annual value of £23. When the lease expired in 1752 Sir Peter let it for £20 p.a. Sir P. Leicester's two rack rents (Appendix 2.3) are just below the annual values. Sir Peter Warburton paid all the taxes for the demesne lands and repaired all the buildings. Account vouchers show that on rack-rented properties in other townships, the tenants paid the taxes and did their repairs but recovered the costs on an annual account against the rent due. So we can say with confidence that all these rack rents were subject to the landlord paying for taxes and repairs. Confirmation that this view of the annual values is correct is provided by the Venables's three-life leasehold with an annual value of £14. In 1754 Sir Peter bought this from his widow in return for an annuity of £12 12s. 0d. (representing the after-tax-and-repair value) and let it in 1756 for £14 rack rent.

There is a note dated 1764 among Aston tax assessments that the annual values used for land tax and poor rates were the same and in 1764 were about two-thirds of the rack rents.

Appleton

The tax assessment folder has a list dated 1744 of names and then three columns of figures headed 'A Mize: An Assessment: Land Tax'. The assessment is at one penny in the pound of annual value and was used to raise tax for the poor and the highways. The annual values derived from this are those shown in Appendices 2.7 to 2.10 inclusive. Most of the 4s. land tax assessments are 1s. in the pound on these values, but not all are.

TABLE 14 *Comparisons of valuations and rack rents, Appleton, 1744*

Leaseholder	Annual value	1744 rack rent
	£	£
Richard Percival, Lower Town	48	50
Joseph Walworth, Higher Town	48	48
Thomas Wilkinson, Higher Town	48	50

There are similar discrepancies to those in the 1741 Aston list.

That these values are close to the rack-rent values current in 1744 is shown by three properties listed in Table 14. Further confirmation is provided by properties that were rack-rented later. In 1748 J. Smith took J. Tomlinson's Yew Tree Farm at the rack rent of £60 p.a., compared with a 1744 annual value of £53. In 1752 Thomas Harper sold his leasehold of Broomfields to Sir Peter and agreed to pay a rack rent of £85 p.a., compared with an annual value in 1744 of £82.

That the 1744 list values may be some decades old, although still the current values of much farmland, is shown by the valuation of Mrs Lydia Badley's freehold (Box 25, Folder 2) when Sir Peter bought it from her daughter in 1751. Mr Robert Badley, who survived her, was paying £100 a year for the two freeholds and the leasehold of the Warrens, valued altogether in the 1744 list at £70. The reason for this is almost certainly that the Warrens – eighty-six acres valued very low at £20 p.a. (under 5s. an acre) – had been improved since it was let on this three-life lease (probably when it was still a rabbit warren) in 1686. The field-by-field valuations of 1764 in Folder 2 show that seventy-nine acres of this land were then valued at an average of 17s. an acre.

Great Budworth

A list dated 1769 shows a valuation for the land tax and the tax at three shillings; an assessment and the poor and highways' tax for the year; a mize, and the church and constable levies. The land-tax valuation and the assessment-implied-valuation both total £600. The values have definitely not kept up with the rising rents of the 1750s and 1760s but were not so far wrong in the 1740s. William Widders took a twenty-one-year lease of Partington's freehold in 1744 at £48 compared with its 'annual value' of £44. When Mr Richard Wrench's lease of Boxhedge expired in 1758 it was let to Peter Pickering at £22 p.a., compared with a valuation of £18 10s. 0d. We have seen earlier the difficulties of valuing gentlemen's houses. The valuation folder contains a note that the rent paid in 1740 on the Brownslane estate – the earlier name of Belmont and its farm – was £74 p.a. for the farmland and £13 10s. 0d. for the house and two closes let separately to Mr Yates, a relation of the Earl of Barrymore. This compares with a tax valuation of only £69. Despite this I have felt these values were sufficiently realistic to include them in Appendices 2.4, 2.5, and 2.6.

Crowley

The only tax assessment of the whole township is dated 1703 and values thirty-four farms at a total of £480, but there is also the tax assessment of the Crowley Lodge farms only in 1752–8 which was prepared in connection with offering these properties for sale in 1759, when a field-by-field valuation was also made by a surveyor. This reveals a very complex situation, because some of the land offered for sale was in the neighbouring township of Antrobus and the family was not selling Hollins Farm, adjoining Crowley, which had lands in both Antrobus and Crowley. However, I calculated that the tax assessment was equal to £0.56 (11s. 2d.) an acre on the Crowley lands and I have used this figure to calculate the approximate value of all the Crowley farms. The land surveyor's valuation of the main Crowley Lodge farm at £83 compared with a tax valuation of £85. The identification of the Crowley farms has been done from the deeds (Boxes 48–61 inclusive) aided by the list of the Mize in 1749. This last is too inaccurate to be used as a valuation.

3. *The land tax in the four townships*

It may be useful to summarize the position on these annual values and the land tax. People other than landowners paid some tax. The excise officer in Great Budworth paid £9 tax when the rate was 4s. in the pound. Tithe owners paid tax and so did shops and those with money at interest (see notes on Appendices 2.1, 2.4, and 2.7). Table 15 sets out the net tax paid

TABLE 15 *Net tax payments*

Township	Landowners' annual value as Table 2		Net land tax at 4/- in the £			Rate on annual values		
	£		£	s.	d.	s. in £		%
						s.	d.	
Aston	1,580		125	4	7	1	7	7.9
Great Budworth	560		39	8	8	1	5	7.0
Appleton	1,459		77	19	0	1	1	5.3
Crowley	753		46	11	5	1	3	6.2

by the landowners. We have seen that these annual values were approximately 10s. per acre in the 1740s. There are field-by-field valuations in Folder 2 made in 1774 for several farms in Aston. These show rental values of nearly £1 an acre. Rents at £1 an acre halved the actual rate of the land tax to 3%–4%.

D. Ginter has decribed the rarity of land tax returns and lists of annual values of properties from before 1780.[60] That the returns and lists on which this study is based can be combined with the maps, rentals and deeds of the properties referred to in the tax assessments is no doubt still more unusual.

APPENDIX 2

Appendix 2 comprises twelve tables, Appendices 2.1 to 2.12, on the following pages. The sources for these tables are described in Appendix 1 and notes 2 and 8.

APPENDIX 2.1 *Aston by Budworth freeholders, 1744*

Freeholder	Modern name of house	Approximate Statute acres	Annual value	Land tax at 4/- in £	Probable tenant	Notes
			£	£ s d		
Forest, William	Feldy Green	50	32	2–2–0	himself	His ancestor bought the estate about 1674. He died 1752.
Leicester, Sir Peter	of Tabley					see Appendix 2.3.
Mann, Edward senior	Nettlegate	25	12	1–3–0	his son Edward Mann, jnr	see also Appendix 2.2. Both properties were in family trusts and had been acquired *c.* 1697.
Daniel, heirs of Sir Samuel	of Over Tabley					see Appendix 2.3.
Vernon, trustees for Mary	Gravestone Farm	48	30	2–12–0	John Vernon, her uncle	Her father died in 1734 when she was 2. She and her mother lived in Knutsford. The Vernons bought the land in 1659.

Walton, Thomas	Litley	135	75	6–10–0	Ottiwell Broom in 1751	Bt 1718. Thos Hall tenant before Broom. Bequeathed in 1755 to Hon. Booth Grey.
	Total	258	149			

Others paying land tax

6 Budworth leaseholders each having fields in Aston		$18\frac{3}{4}$		1–13–0		
	Corn tithe		52	4–0–0		
	Vicar's tithe		7	12–9		

APPENDIX 2.2   *Aston by Budworth: Sir Peter Warburton's three-life leaseholders, 1749*

Leaseholder	Modern name of house	Approximate Statute acres	Annual value	Land tax at 4/- in £	Total annual rent	Probable tenant	Notes
			£ 30	£ s d 2–2–0	£ s d 2–9–0	*Peter Buckley	P. Buckley was married to Catherine Amery, daughter and heiress of Ann.
Amery, Ann, widow	West Feldy	47					
Baker, John, gent.	Lower Feldy Green	63	56	4–2–0	4–1–0	Jonathan Beswick	He lived in Kingsley, Cheshire and had married Emm Gleave, the heiress of this property in 1731. She was the sister of Thomas Eaton (see Appendix 2.11), mariner, of Crowley and had married John Gleave about 1725. He died 1730. His father Robert Gleave had farmed the Gore 1718–29. He and his son John had bought these two properties.
	Towngate	13					
Barlow, William	All Fours	16	13	1–3–0	1–2–6	let	Not resident?
Berry, Charles	Stonegate Cottage	2	3	2–0	2–0	part Berry?	Part Peter Sharman – a farmer?
Berry, Jonathan	Cottage at Moss End (demolished)	1	–	–	2–6	part himself?	Part Seddon family? See Table 8.

56

Birchall, James[†]	Cradles Crossfield	14 28	37	2–16–0	4–4–10 *himself	see also his freehold in Crowley (Appendix 2.11). He married Mary Vernon, cousin of the freeholders of Gravestone Farm, Aston (Appendix 2.1). Her family had had at least one of these leases since 1688. Farming up to 1752. Died 1765.
Brown, executors of Joseph	Feldy Green Cottage	35	23	1–12–0	19–0 let	This lease ended on the death of Samuel Glover in 1751 (see this Table). Joseph Brown owned the lease and probably farmed until his death in 1746. This farm let for £20 p.a. in 1752.
Darlington, George	in Arley Park (demolished)	12	16	1–4–0	1–1–10 let	not resident? Let in 1743 to Isaac Houghton. See Table 8.
Dewsbury, Robert[†]	Old Shop East Feldy	12 44	42	13–0 1–19–3	1–3–11 *himself 1–17–0 Samuel his eldest son, born 1715	He died in 1752 and left the Old Shop, his family's ancient holding, to Samuel and Feldy Green to his next son John and both were expected to farm.
Forest, John[†]	Guidepost	32	19	1–12–0	19–6 *himself	
Glover, Samuel	Hollin Hall (demolished) in Arley Park	32	19	1–4–0	1–10–0 John Robinson the leaseholder	He was retired and living in Gt Budworth (see Henshall, Appendix 2.5). He also had leaseholds under Sir Peter Leicester in Aston (Appendix 2.3), a freehold in Crowley (Appendix 2.11) and a freehold in Antrobus. He died 1751.
	Brettons (demolished) by Hilltop	45	20	1–14–0	1–8–6 Mathew Darlington	
Handley, Thomas	Stonegate	5	8	14–0	11–7 *himself	Also farming other land? Died 1754.
Heath, John	Royal Oak	3	7	9–4	8–6 let	Resident in Budworth?
Hind, Richard	Cottage at Moss End (demolished)	–	–	–	5–0 himself and family	Labourer aged 68 who built the cottage in 1708. Some of his children and grandchildren lived there with him.

Hunt, Martha	beside East Feldy	8	7	13–0	13–0 let	Widow, probably not resident.
Littler, Thomas	Crabtree Cottage	5	10	13–0	8–6 let	Thomas Litler of Gt Budworth, carpenter.
Mann, Edward senior[†]	Arleymoss	49	28	2–4–0	2–7–9 *himself	See also Appendix 2.1. He was at least 65. The farming was being controlled on both properties by Ann, widow of Edward Mann junior, who had died in 1746.
Moore, Ann, widow[†]	opposite Georges Lane (demolished)	32	21	2–0–0	2–16–1 Peter Sharman?	Probably non-resident after 1751. Sold lease to Peter Sharman 1752. He sold to Sir Peter Warburton in 1755/6.
Okell, Thomas	Ashes	34	27	2–2–0	1–3–6 Ralph Kinsey?	A minor till 1749. Not resident till 1760?
Partington, John	Cottage nr Hilltop (demolished)	8	5	7–0	7–0 *himself	
Pickering, Samuel	A cottage, now Bate House	–	–	–	2–4 himself	A sawyer and carpenter born 1703. See Table 8.
Richardson, Richard	Moss End Cottage	1	2¼	3–0	5–0 himself	Miller. See Table 8.
Robinson, John	Birchbrook in Arley Park (demolished)	28	19	1–10–0	1–10–0 *himself	He was also tenant of Glover's Hollin Hall leasehold and Arley demesne land. Died 1750.
Seddon, Elizabeth	2–3 Hield Cottages	–	–	–	1–6 herself?	Probably a poor labouring widow, see Table 8. After her death in 1753, cottage let to overseers of poor at £1–10–0 p.a.
Shakeshaft, Hugh	Georges Lane Farm	10	9	18–0	12–0 let	Not resident in Aston. Thomas Prescot may have been the tenant.
Starkey, James	Hilltop	41	33	2–9–0	1–16–8 *himself for part of the land	see also Budworth leasehold of Thomas Starkey (Appendix 2.5). James and John, who may have been brothers, were both farming on this land.

Venables, William	Crofton	20	14	1–0–0	1–1–0	himself	Sir Peter Warburton took over this farm when he died in 1753 and paid the widow £12–12–0 p.a. for her life interest.
Walton, James	Churn Cottage	6	5	4–4	5–9	*himself	Also farming 53 acres in demesne when J. Robinson died, see Appendix 2.12.
Wilcoxen, Jane, widow	Pinfold	26	20	1–9–0	1–19–6	*herself	Her husband died 1748, leaving her with 4 children under 16.
Winstanley, Thomas	Longridge	–	–	2–0	5–4	himself	See also widow Winstanley (Table 8).
Wood, John	in Arley Park (demolished)	24	16	1–4–0	1–11–4	*himself	
Wright, Isaac	opposite Litley (demolished)	34	16	1–8–0	2–1–9	*himself	
	Totals	730	525¼				

Notes:

†These farms were still occupied by someone of the same name as the leaseholder pre-1700. Birchall had married Vernon, the pre-1700 occupier. Others may have descended through women.

*These 13 farms and smallholdings, out of the total of 24 listed, were being worked by a member of the leaseholder's family.

APPENDIX 2.3 *Aston by Budworth: Sir Peter Leicester and Sir Samuel Daniel's leaseholders, 1740s*

Leaseholder	Modern name of house	Approximate statute acres	annual value	Land tax at 4/- in £	Total annual rent	probable tenant	Notes
			£	£ s d	£ s d		
Leicester Manor of Hield							
Anderton, Thomas	Hield House	67	60	4–6–0	3–0–0	Mr Dutton	T. Anderton probably lived at Hield with his niece Ann Pimlow (see Appendix 2.4) till he died in 1748.

Robinson, John, Mr	beside Hield	43	33	2–8–0	1–19–0 John Smallwood	Lived in Manchester? Tenant in 1715
Worrall, Hugh	Cottage beside Hield	8	7	9–0	12–0 himself	Farming.

Leicester Manor of Wethale

Glover, Samuel	Wathall Farm North of Wathall (demolished)	49 40	50	2–12–0 1–16–0	2–0–2 Peter Barber then Mary Barber	see also his leaseholds (Appendix 2.2). His family had been on the Tabley estate in the 17th century and had held one of these leases since 1697.
demesne land	Batefield (no house)	13?	15	1–3–0	13–0–0 let	Rack rent of £13.
Key, Richard	Kays	75	40	3–9–4	2–6–2 Wm Toft	Family on farm since at least 1697.
Toft, William	beside Kays	45	27	2–2–0	1–10–0 himself	Family on farm since at least 1697.
Richardson, Richard	Yewtree	16?	18	1–10–0	15-0-0 himself	Rack rent £15. Clockmaker – one of his clocks is at Arley. An old man by 1740s, probably getting someone to farm for him.
Cooke, John	Cottage on Bateheath (demolished)	1	2¼	3–0	6–0 Samuel Cooke	See Table 8 for S. Cooke.
	Totals	357	252¼			

Executors of Sir S. Daniel

Spragg, Thomas	Lands End	17	9	19–0	1–4–0 himself	Died 1753.
Tovey, Ruth, widow	Cann Lane Farm	7	5	8–4	9–0 herself	Born 1662. Land probably being worked by Ralph Kinsey: see Appendix 2.12.
	Totals	24	14			

APPENDIX 2.4 *Great Budworth freeholders, 1749*

Freeholder	Modern name of house	Statute acres	Approximate Annual value	Land tax at 4/- in £	Probable tenant	Notes
			£	£ s d		
Cooke, Mary	10–14 High St	7	10	13–4		Mother of Samuel who bought the lease of 15 High St in 1749?
Leicester, Sir Peter	of Tabley	50				See the separate list of his three-life lease-holders (Appendix 2.6).
Partington, Thomas	Brownslow House	62	44	3–6–0	William Widders	His father, Thomas Partington of Manchester, gent, bought this farm as an investment in 1724. This Thomas, a clockmaker of Manchester, sold in 1749.
Pimlow, Ann, widow	Goldmine Farm	38	31¾	2–16–0	James Pimlow, brother-in-law	Married in 1738 and widowed in 1740. Her father-in-law William Pimlow bought almost all the land in 1724. See also her leasehold (Appendix 2.5).
Slaughter, Thomas	Belmont and Brownslow Farm	109	69	4–7–0	let to John and Thomas Willet?	Brother-in-law to Sir Peter Warburton, 4th Bt, he inherited this on the death of Sir George, 3rd Bt, in 1743. He was living in Aston Park, Sir George bought it in 1739. T. Slaughter sold to Hon. John Smith Barry, who built Belmont, in 1749.
Wrench, Richard, of Davenham	Crowsnest	9	8	12–8	Peter Barlow	His father-in-law, Peter Dutton of Gt Budworth, put this land in trust on the marriage of his daughter Sarah to R. Wrench. Sold 1758.
Selby, Richard, vicar of Gt Budworth	Church and vicarage	4	4	5–4	–	Tax was charged on the value of the house and the vicar's tithes in Great Budworth township, which he collected himself. Generally, tithes paid land tax in their own townships.
Totals		276	166¾			

Others paying land tax

Mr Deacon of Comberbach – mercer – for a shop?		10–8	
Corn tithe		1–7–4	
Excise Officer		9–0–0	

APPENDIX 2.5 *Great Budworth: Sir Peter Warburton's leaseholders, 1745*

Leaseholder	Modern name of house	Approximate Statute acres	Approximate Annual value £	Land tax at 4/- in £ £ s d	Total annual rent £ s d	Age	Place of abode	Notes
Acton, Mary	15 High St "y"	9	7	10–0	15–1	57	Budworth	The only 'life' in being. Widow who had 4 daughters. Sold in 1749. See Cooke freehold. (Appendix 2.4).
Anderton, John	Fairfield Cottages	7	7	8–8	13–7	40	Warrington	
Burgess, Alice, widow	50 Church St "k"	4	6¼	7–0	10–0	40	Budworth	Her husband George, a gardener, died March 1745. The Durling family had owned 51 High St since 1690 but they sold and went to London, 1736.
	51 High St "i" (now George & Dragon)	6			8–10			
Burgess, George	on edge of Heath	–	–	0–0–8	2–8	42	Budworth	Tailor. Lived with his wife, 40, and son, 19.
Dutton, William	16 High St "d"	2	3	4–0	11–6	49	Budworth	This house had its kitchen across the road, in what is now the barn of no. 59. There were two houses at 45 Church St.
	45 Church St "n"	9	6	8–4	10–0			
Dutton, trustees of Thomas	37, 38, 39 Church St "r" 34, 35, 36 School Lane "s"	5	6	7–6	17–7	29	Budworth	2 or 3 houses. The Dutton family had been leading citizens of Budworth in the 17th century. A cattle dealer.
Eaton, Abdulla	3 Dene Cottages	3	3	3–0	8–6	65	Budworth	The heir to this property was Rev. John Eaton, 40, of Brasenose College, Oxford.
Goulden, John	32–33 School Lane "t"	8	7	9–4	15–0	46	Budworth	Only one house then. Living with his son, 23.

Heath, John	42 Church St "o" Barn or school "p"	3	5	5–4	9–8		Budworth	There may have been a school in the Barn, which had been a separate holding.
Heath, William	demolished to straighten road by Dene Cottages	–	–	–	2–4	52	?	
Henshall, John	48 & 49 Church St (Hough's Farm) "l"	14	12	16–0	1–2–6	42	Over Peover	His mother, 71, probably lived here, as also Samuel Dutton (see his Aston leaseholds and Crowley freehold). In 1751, on the death of S. Dutton, Henshall sold to Henry Hough, whose family held it into the 19th century.
Hough, Joseph	21 High St "v"	21	17	1–2–8	1–15–7	54	Budworth	His son Henry, 30, was living with him and they were farming.
	Wolfe House (on Heath)	3	3	4–0				
Hazlehurst, George	(17) 18 High St "x"	–	–	0–8	2–4	35		
Horton, Martha	demolished (by Heath)	2	2	3–4	6–4	70	Wincham	
Littler, John	62 High St "a"	–	–	–	4–8	45?	Pickmere	His brother-in-law Samuel Fryer lived there with his family.
Littler, Thomas	22–24 High St "u"	1	1½	2–0	4–10	38	Budworth	2 cottages then on the site. Littler lived in one and Stones had a lease of the other. See also his Aston leasehold.
Littler, William	53 High St "g"	6	6	8–8	10–5	22	Budworth	These three Littlers were probably related and all carpenters.

Marsh, Joseph	Part of 41 Church St "q"	–	1½	2–0	4–10	38?	Budworth	He was farming, assisted by his mother, 54, a son, 21, and a daughter, 18.
	Reidfield and barn	27	14	18–8	1–12–8			
Mee, Ann	52 High St "h"	22	20	1–6–8	14–10	35	Peover	Sister or wife of Richard Mee, gent, of Peover. Tenant Revd Simon Mills. Managed by Thomas Gorst, lawyer, and steward of Tabley estate.
Nickson, William	demolished cottage on Heath edge	8	7	9–0	9–4	52	Thelwall	
Pimlow, Ann	60–61 High St "b"	15	8¾	11–10	1–4–6	35	Aston by Budworth	Probably living with her uncle Thomas Anderton at Hield where she lived before marriage. Her brother-in-law James farming. See Appendix 2.4.
Percival, William	19–20 High St "w" 46–47 Church St "m"	13	11¾	15–4	1–2–4	40	Budworth	Carpenter-builder living with his wife, 35, and daughter, 19.
Pimlow, Hannah	Cock Lane Farm and smithy at	7	5¼	6–8	15–6		Witton, where her late husband lived	Widow of James, died 1741. She died 1748. The property was left to her son by an earlier marriage, John Okell, 23.
Shakeshaft, Richard	54 and 57 High St "f"	–	2	1–4	7–4	21	London	Vintner in Leadenhall Market. There were 2 houses on the site.
Starkey, Richard	demolished cottage in road by Dene Cottages	1	1½	1–4	5–2	42	Norley	

Starkey, Thomas	Heath Cottage and smithy beside	26	12¾	17–4	1–9–5		?	Related to James and John who were farming Hilltop in Aston, to which some of this land adjoined. They were probably farming it all.
Thomason, William	59 High St "c"	7	7	7–6	15–0	54	Budworth	Farming. Only life in lease.
Venables, executors of Thomas, for his son Peter	Sandicroft	30	18½	1–8–0	1–7–9	14	?	Not farming himself.
Underwood, Alice, widow since 1728	Brownslow Cottage	17	12½	18–4	19–0	50	Budworth	Her daughter Catherine, 20, the heiress of the property, married Thomas Widders in 1749 and they built up a large farm.
Wrench, Mr Richard	Boxhedge	31	18½	1–9–4	1–7–9		Davenham	See also Appendix 2.4. This was also acquired through his wife.
Willett, John	The Cock Inn	29	30½	2–1–8	2–15–2	35	Budworth	His wife was aged 30 and his son 14.
Yate, Mr Hamlet	Old Hall 58 High St "e"	43	42	3–5–4	2–12–11	74	Budworth	See also his freehold in Crowley (Appendix 2.11). He farmed a small area (10 to 20 acres) himself and let the rest.
	Budworth Heath Farm	88	35¼	2–12–4	5–2–9			
Yarwood, William	Quebec Cottage	1	–	–	2–2	58	Budworth	Labourer in gardens at Arley Hall.
	Totals	468	340½					

Note: The letters "a" to "y" in this table refer to the village plan in Map 7. See Appendix 3.

APPENDIX 2.6 *Great Budworth: Sir Peter Leicester's leaseholders, c.1756*

Leaseholder	Modern name of house	Approximate Statute acres	Annual value	Land tax at 4/- in £	Total annual rent
			£ 9	s d	£ s d
*French, William	Surgery, Southbank	10	9	11–0	1–1–9
Green, John	27–28 Southbank Westgate	11	10	7–4	9–0
Heath, Samuel	Southbank House and Cottage House	5	4	6–0	12–0
Heath, William	Westage Farm	4	4	5–4	7–0
Highfield, Sarah	Cock Lane Cottages	–	–	–	8–0
Hough, Henry	9 The Mount	11	10	14–4	16–6
Hulme, John	4–5 The Mount	3	3½	4–4	10–0
Pimlow, Elizabeth	7–8 The Mount	10	8½	11–10	12–0
Robey, William	Part 41 Church St	–	–	–	2–6
Thomason William	40 Church St	2	2½	2–0	7–8
	Totals	56	51½		

*Two houses.

Notes:
1. This schedule is substantially less reliable than the schedules of freeholders and Warburton leaseholders because the Tabley archive is largely uncatalogued and unsorted.
2. The area includes about 6 acres in Aston by Budworth.
3. The ten names are correct. There were about 50 acres of Leicester land in Budworth and the houses were located in Southbank, The Mount, etc., as shown, but the identification of particular tenants with their land and its value is unreliable.

Freeholder	Modern name of house	Approximate Statute acres	Annual value £	Land tax at 4/- in £ £ s d	Probable tenant	Notes
Badley, Mrs Lydia	Bellfield Bate's Mill, Stockton Heath	85 7	50	See Appendix 2.8	Thomas Sutton	She was born Lydia Southern in 1701 and inherited the Bellfields estate and the Warrens leasehold (Appendix 2.8) from her father, whose family had owned it since 17th century. Her first husband John Bate owned the Stockton Heath freehold and leasehold (Appendix 2.8) and more land in Latchford. Robert Radley was her second husband and they may have lived in Stockton Heath. She died about 1749, and all the land was sold by her daughter in 1751.
Bent, Cheney, Dr of Physic, of Shrewsbury	Appleton Hall (now demolished)	48	27	1–8–0	Joseph Mills	This estate was sold by the Rycroft family, who had owned it in 1666, to Theophilus Bent of Warrington, maltster, in the early 1740s, from whom it passed to Dr Bent. He soon sold to Matthew Lyon, whose family built Appleton Hall in the early 19th century.
Birchall, William	Brow Farm	42	22	1–2–0	himself	Probably 2nd son of Thomas, brother of James of Crowley and Aston (Appendices 2.1, 2.2). He acquired this estate and the neighbouring leasehold in Appleton (Appendix 2.10) in 1733 from the Twiss family, to whom he was related. They had owned them from the 1690s or earlier.
Cartwright, Dainteth	Dainteth's Farm	40	20	1–2–0	Henry Cartwright	He inherited aged 3 on the death of his grandfather John Dainteth in 1739. The Dainteths had owned the estate since the 16th century or earlier.
Clare, Joseph	Birchtree Farm and a cottage beside (demolished)	41	16½	17–0	himself	Born in 1699, he inherited from his father in 1727.
Dudley or Dudlow, Samuel	demolished at Dudlow Green	10	6	5–0	himself	His family had been owners since 1666 or earlier. Value includes small leasehold (Appendix 2.8).

Eaton, George of the Pole, Antrobus	The Hurst land on Cann Lane	110	40 8	2–0–0 8–8	Thomas Sankey	The largest landowner among the numerous Eaton family freeholders in the area, his estate was 500–1000 acres.
	Great Shepcroft	113	48	2–12–4	let	These farms came to his ancestor by marriage at the end of the 17th century.
Leigh, Rev. Thomas	Hillfoot Farm	76	40	2–4–0	Thomas Sutton	Uncle of George Leigh of Oughtrington, Lymm. He bought the farm as an investment in 1728. Rector of Stoke Bruern, Northants.
Middleton, John	Hillcliffe House in London Road	79	39	2–0–0	Thomas Dobson?	His ancestors had held part of the land since the early 17th century and had bought part from the Morris family of Grappenhall in early 18th century.
Stubs, Charles	Dennow	36	20	1–7–0	let?	He was charged 5/- extra land tax for his 'money at interest'.
Sutton, Peter	Woodside Farm (demolished)	19	12	12–8	John Rathbourne	His father Thomas, bodice-maker of Crompton, Lancs, bought it as an investment in 1717. Sold 1752.
Wainwright, Thomas (trustee)	Baptist Chapel	2	–	no tax		
Totals North of Stockton Heath		708 120	348½ 71			The corn tithe in the whole of Appleton paid £4–0–0 land tax. The vicar's tithe in the whole of Appleton paid £0–10–0 land tax.
		828	419½			

Notes:
1. In addition to the above freehold land there was an area of about 120 acres between the two Stockton Heath commons and the river Mersey. I have no map, deeds or rentals for this area because only two small areas were ever owned by the Warburtons: Mrs Badley's Bate's Mill, as above, and the Saracen's Head, at Wilderspool.
2. Peter Brooke, esq., of Mere had freeholds which 'lay in a string' between Walton and Latchford. One of 22 acres was let to the Brown family and another to Rev. Thomas Moss. John Ansdale also had a freehold of at least 20 acres. Below is a list of the 13 Taxpayers of 1744 to which I have added notes from a list of the 23 freeholders who had a share in the commons in 1765. We can safely envisage some wharves on the Mersey at Wilderspool beside the malt kiln, brewery and Saracen's Head. The rest of the houses lined the road from Wilderspool to Stockton Heath and the north side of both commons (see Map 5).

APPENDIX 2.7.2 *Appleton Lower Town freeholders between Stockton Heath commons and river Mersey*

Tax payer or other name	Annual value	Land tax at 4/- in £	*Notes
	£	£ s d	
Blackburn, Mrs Sarah	3	8–0	3 acres in 1765 valued at £13 6s. 9d. Wife or mother of John Blackburn, esq., of Orford?
Brown, Mary	18	19–4	As well as the 22 acres sold by Brooke of Mere to Ann Dutton in 1761 there were three Brown family freeholds in 1765 totalling about 5 acres valued at £10 10s. 5d. See also John Brown's leasehold (Appendix 2.8).
Brown, William senior	2½	2–0	
Brown, William junior	¾	–	
Burgess, widow	3	2–8	Thomas Ford tenant?
Crossbrook tenement	2	3–0	Presumably where the road to Walton crossed the brook.
Dunbabin, Margaret	1	1–0	
Lyon, Mr Matthew for			These three are bracketed together as 'Harts and Com'. See also Mr Lyon's leasehold (Appendix 2.8). In 1765 'Messrs Thos and Jeffrey Hart' owned 13 acres valued at £18 17s. 10d. and 'Harts and Co' had 4 acres valued at £12 11s. 8d.
Cartwrights for	4	4–0	
Longshaws	4	8–0	
Longshaw, John	1¼	1–0	
Peacock, John	7½	10–0	In 1765 he had 13 acres valued at £17 0s. 10d. on the Walton Road.
Skins, Joseph	6	10–0	Innkeeper, died 1745.
Yates, Richard	18	18–0	Probably tenant of Ansdale. Peter Harrison, who acquired this freehold, had 20 acres in 1765 on the Walton Road beside two Yates family cottages.
Total	71		

*The value of agricultural land in 1765 was under £1 per acre so higher values probably indicate commercial use.

APPENDIX 2.8 *Appleton Lower Town leaseholders, 1744*

Leaseholder	Modern name of house	Approximate Statute acres	Annual value	Land tax at 4/- in £	Total annual rent	Notes
			£	£ s d	£ s d	
Badley, Mrs Lydia	Old Warrens, now golf course	86	20	3–12–0	1–7–10	Tax payments include freeholds (Appendix 2.7). Thomas Southern farmed the land. John Bate, cheese factor, who died 1728, probably did not, and Richard Badley, gentleman, almost certainly did not.
	Old Stockton Heath House, now Orchard St and Mitchell St	50	24	1–4–0	1–14–4	
Bate, Ralph	demolished on Dudlow Green	48	30	1–12–0	2–3–6	Younger brother of Mrs Badley's first husband John Bate. Their father owned both freehold and leasehold at his death in 1724. Probably resident in the area but not farming.
Brown, John	on Walton Road	2	1	2–0	2–4	Demolished cottage beside his family's freehold/leasehold.
Barker, Arthur	demolished cottages beside Mrs Badley's Stockton Heath House	–	2	2–0	2–0	
Cosgrave, Otho		–	1	–	?	Leased from J. Middleton in 1744. Bought by Warburton 1750. He lived in Lancashire and let this cottage.
Dudley, Samuel	intake beside his freehold	2	1		3–4	Taxed with freehold (Appendix 2.7).
Ellam, Richard	demolished on Hatton Road	10	6	4–4	4–4	Tailor?
Golden, Thomas	The Hilal, Stockton Heath	–	5	4–0	4–0	Blacksmith's shop.
Harper, Thomas	Old Broomfields, now school, etc.	172	82	4–5–6	4–11–0	Largest resident farmer.

Freeholder	Modern name of house					Notes
Jennings, Joshua	land nr Dainteths	15	5	4–0	6–6	His father had bought the lease about 1686. Henry Cartwright of Dainteths was his tenant. He died 1754. He was illiterate.
Lyon, Mr Matthew	Old Mill Farm	2	6	9–4	3–0	He had inherited it from his uncle Matthew Page. The high value per acre suggests commercial use, perhaps an inn. George Simcock tenant.
Moss, Rev. Thomas	Wilderspool	–	10½	10–8	1–2–6	Malt kiln and Saracen's Head public house. The high value and tax may include the land he was leasing from Brooke of Mere.
Percival, Richard	Hillside Farm	124	48	2–12–4	50–0–0	Rack rent £50. Resident farmer.
Shakeshaft, Samuel	demolished cottages, Bridge Lane	4	2	3–4	3–6	
Sutton, Peter	intake beside freehold	1			1–0	Value included with freehold (Appendix 2.7).
Twambrooks, Mrs	Little Shepcroft	73	24	1–14–0	1–12–8	Tenant John Gleave junior.
Whitlow, Peter and John	Old Pinfold, now Dingle Lodge	26	20	1–1–0	19–0	Resident farmers?
	Totals	615	287½			

APPENDIX 2.9 *Appleton Higher Town freeholders, 1744*

Freeholder	Modern name of house	Approximate Statute acres	Annual value	Land tax at 4/- in £	Probable tenant	Notes
			£	£ s d		
Bate, James?	unidentified	8?	4	1–6	Wright?	'School House' in tax return. Grappenhall school lands at Wrights Green?
Crosby, Mr John	Stud Farm	30	18	17–4	J. Stringer	His ancestors had owned this since at least the 16th century. Sold 1754.

Owner	Property			Value	Tenant	Notes
Dutton, Roger	demolished cottage in Cann Lane	–	–	–	–	Valued with his leasehold (Appendix 2.10) for tax.
Egerton, John, esq.	Bradley Hall land at Wrights Green	152 5	70	4–5–0	John, Bostock	This estate, which included a farm in Crowley (Appendix 2.11), had belonged to the Gregg family and came to Egerton with his wife Elizabeth Brock of Upton.
Hewitt, Joseph	Hattons Farm, Pepper St	20	12	12–0	himself?	There was a windmill on the site. The Hattons were here in 1666. J. Hewitt replaced widow Hatton in 1732 and was succeeded by T. Hatton in 1760.
Minshall, Thomas	Beech House Hatton House	11	9	7–0	?	Bought about 1724.
Moss, Revd Thomas, fellow of the collegiate church of Manchester	Cross Farm Walnut Tree Farm Green Lane Farm demolished cottage, Cann Lane ——— 127	68 26 32 1	74	3–10–0	unknown at this period	James Moss and his son John, of Manchester, woollen drapers, bought this between 1678 and 1707 from the Millingtons, who had bought half of it from the Watts in 1667. Revd Thomas was 2nd son of John Moss.
Pendlebury, John	Patch and Wrights Green Cottages	9			Edward Twam-brookes,	Value included in Twambrook's leasehold (Appendix 2.10). He bought it from Pendlebury about this period.
Stretch, Josiah	Dairy Farm	28	15	18–0	?	Value includes his leasehold (Appendix 2.10). He bought it in 1741 from the Grimsditch family, owners since the 17th century.
Shaw, Peter Stringfellow, Henry	These may be names of tenants	6 6	5–0 6–0			
	Totals	390 *50 ——— 440	214			

*Note: In addition to these freehold acreages there were 40 acres held by Thomas Taylor in 1765 at Cann Lane Farm and 10 acres held by Thomas Pigott of Mosswood Hall, but I do not know who owned them in 1744.

APPENDIX 2.10 *Appleton Higher Town three-life leaseholders, 1744*

Leaseholder	Modern name of house	Approximate Statute acres	Annual value	Land tax at 4/- in £	Total annual rent	Notes
			£ 20	£ s d 1–0–0	£ s d 2–15–4	
Birchall, Joshua	Nook Farm	42	20	1–0–0	2–15–4	
Birchall, William	Wood Farm (part)	27	15	15–4	16–0	Resident farmer. Probably nephew of James Birchall of Crowley and Aston. He bought this and freehold from his Twiss relations in 1733.
Brearley, John	Cottage in Pepper St	2	1	8	2–8	Demolished.
Caldwell, John	Thornbrow Farm Appleton Thorn pub	67	28	1–10–0	2–2–9	Resident farmer and alehouse keeper.
Caldwell, Joseph	Beehive Farm	43	20	1–0–0	1–11–5	Resident farmer.
Clare, Peter	Burleyheyes	181	52	2–18–0	4–4–0	Resident farmer.
Dutton, Roger	land only	23	18	17–4	13–1	Value includes freehold (Appendix 2.9). He also had land in Stretton, where he lived.
Davies, John	Cabbage Hall	2	2	2–0	5–8	
Jackson, Peter	Wood Farm (part)	31	16	15–4	15–3	Samuel Webb tenant?
Knowles, Gabriel	Barleycastle	39	16	18–0	1–13–4	His family's ancient tenement. Born in 1680s. Farmed Turner's freehold in Crowley (Appendix 2.11). Died 1754.
Knowles, Matthew	Tanyard	61	28	1–10–0	1–19–0	Died 1745, when his son, Thomas, known as 'Tanner Knowles', succeeded.
Moss, Revd Thos.	land only	10			7–6	Enclosed on 3 sides by his freehold (Appendix 2.9) and taxed with it.

Percival, James jnr	Spenheath	6	5	5–0	4–6	Smithy. House was School Cottage.
Percival, James snr	Wrights Green House	1			3–0	Thomas Percival, tenant.
Reddish, Thomas	Crofton	7	6	5–0	4–8	Demolished?
Royle, Peter	demolished nr Walnut Tree	13	12	12–0	11–4	May have been tenant of part of Taylors 1765 freehold (Appendix 2.9, note).
Shakeshaft, Margaret	between Barleycastle and Tanyard	14	9	14–6	1–6–0	Demolished. Land tax includes 5s. on money at interest. Elderly spinster. Let.
Stretch, Josiah	land beside freehold	1			1–0	Valued and taxed with freehold (Appendix 2.9).
Taylor, John		1	1	4	1–10	Resident.
Taylor, widow	Cann Lane Farm land only	½	6	5–0	2–0	Value and tax likely to include part of Taylor's 1765 freehold (Appendix 2.9, note).
Tomlinson, Timothy	Witherwing	95	42	2–4–0	2–11–8	Probably let. He surveyed and mapped the commons in Appleton in 1756.
Tomlinson, Jonathon	Yewtree	106	53	2–14–0	1–17–7	Probably let to Thomas Hampson. Tomlinson lived in Carrington.
Twambrookes, Edward	Dingle Farm	89	40	2–0–0	2–17–3	Value includes Pendlebury's freehold (Appendix 2.9), of which he was tenant. Brother-in-law of William Birchall.
Twambrookes, Thomas	School Farm	27	15	14–0	1–4–2	The son Thomas was probably farming his widowed mother's land as well as his own.
Twambrookes, widow	Laurel Cottage, Pepper St	40	17	19–0	1–1–9	
Wallworth, Joseph	Old Farm	123	48	2–12–0	48–0–0	Rack or farm rent £48. Resident farmer.
Wilkinson, Thomas	Booth's Farm	98	48	2–12–0	50–0–0	Rack or farm rent £50. Resident farmer.

Wilson, John	Gibraltar Cottage	1	1	2–0	10
Witter, John	Post Office	21	14	14–0	17–5
Wright, John	at Wright's Green	1	4	2–4	2–6	Demolished. Sold to John Caldwell? Clockmaker?
	Totals	1168½	537		

Note: Wallworth and Wilkinson held at rack rents, not on three-life leases

APPENDIX 2.11 *Crowley freeholders, 1749*

Freeholder	Modern name of house	Approximate Statute acres	Approximate Annual value	Probable tenant	Notes
Birchall, James trustees of his marriage settlement	Sandilands	55	£ 31	Thomas Deane	A farmer living in Aston. He was given this farm on his marriage in 1705 by his father, who had bought it in 1699. His only daughter and heiress married Revd John Boardman, rector of Grappenhall, and they may have enjoyed the income. It was originally 3 farms.
Brotherton, Revd Thos	Crowley Grange	41		W. Shakeshaft,	His ancestors had owned this land since 17th century. He married Ann Chandler, daughter of the bishop of Durham.
	Rangehead	42		J. Plant	
		83	46		
Davenport, Ralph	Crowley Lodge	132		J. Carter	He was the grandson, aged 23, of Ralph Davenport of Chorley, Lancs., merchant, who bought these 4 farms between 1727 and 1732. He also lived in Chorley. Hollins Farm was actually in Antrobus but some land was in Crowley.
	Leathers Farm	117		J. Dale	
	Land only (now in Arley Park)	33		E. Savage	
(in trust for his mother)	Hollins Farm	30		?	
		312	175		

Name	House/place			Tenant	Notes
Eaton, John, of Liverpool, trustee for Thomas Eaton, mariner, and family	Parkmoss	74	41	J. Jolley	His father, also Thomas Eaton, had inherited and farmed at least half of this land. He put it in trust by his will of 1728, his son, the mariner, being under age. The mariner sold in 1752.
Egerton, John, esq.	Galebrook	34	19	Edw. Jackson, (24 acres); Leigh (8 acres)	In the 17th century it was part of the estate of Gregg of Bradley Hall, Appleton, and came to the Egertons via 2 heiresses. See below for Edward Jackson's freehold. It is possible that these two tenants had three-life leases.
Glover, Samuel, of Aston and Gt Budworth	no house? beside Wm Knowles's land	10?	6	Wm Massey	He may have inherited this land from his uncle Samuel Glover of High Legh. He left it by his will of 1751 to his nephew William Knowles (this table).
Haslehurst, John	The Firs	19	11	?	His ancestors had leased this land since at least 1658 and owned it since 1697. He had a joinery business and lived in Antrobus.
Jackson, Edward	Reedside	7	4	himself	He represented Crowley in Gt Budworth parish vestry and probably lived on and farmed this land, which he bought in 1731. He had a little more land adjoining in Antrobus and the lease of 24 acres of Egerton's Galebrook farm (this table). Died in 1757 in Budworth.
Knowles, William	Reedgate Hades Nook	48?	27	?	His ancestors had owned this land since 1614. His father died in 1744 when he was about 15. Probably not farming. There were 58 acres after the Glover bequest (this table).
Heyward, John	Crowley Green	37	21	himself	His ancestors had lived here for at least a generation before they bought in 1697. He was the only freeholder farming in the 1757 list of tithe payers.
Hough, Thomas	Firtree	127		Thomas Key,	A Quaker farmer whose ancestors had farmed on the Warburton's Sutton Weaver manor since 16th century and he still did. He had bought all this land. Firtree was originally 3 farms.
	Poolsplatt say	50		Thomas Haslehurst	
		177	99		

Peover School, trustees of	Park Farm	57	32	J. Beckett	Bought from Thos. Eaton in 1724 and Edward Jackson in 1735 for £610, as an investment.
Rutter, Richard, of Moore, Cheshire	Crowley Hall	172	96	T. Broxton	A gentleman with an estate of 500–1000 acres which he had by inheritance from 17th century or earlier. Originally it had been several farms.
Rylands, Peter	Caldwells Gate	76	43	T. Wright	His ancestors were here before 1657 when they bought half this property. They bought the other half in 1699 and his father farmed. He was born in 1697, inherited in 1727 and probably farmed when young. By 1749 he probably lived in Great Budworth. He sold in 1762.
Sutton, John	Pennypleck	9	5	?	House and 9 acres in Crowley with probably more land in High Legh.
Turner, Mr Matthew	Galemoss	36	20	?	Bought by his father John from Gabriel Knowles around 1730 (see Appendix 2.10) Both father and son were surgeons in Liverpool.
Yate, Hamlet	Garland Hall Smithy Farm in Arley Village Crowley Chapel House	102 16 19		J. Dawson W. Robinson { J. Garland J. Heyward	A lawyer in his 70s. He was steward of the Arley estate 1689–1733 and was now living in Gt Budworth where he had leaseholds. He bought this land between 1712 and 1737.
		137	77		
	Total	1,343	753		

APPENDIX 2.12 *Aston by Budworth: Sir Peter Warburton's demesne lands at farm or rack rents, 1749*

Occupier	Location	Statute acres	Approximate Annual value	Farm or rack rent	Notes
			£	£ s d	
himself	Arley Hall	393	215	–	About half the land was near the house and the rest in the area of the later New Farm.
Amery, Ann, widow	Gore Banks	6	2½	2–10–0	No house. See Appendix 2.2.
Barnett, William	Great Faulters	39	18	18–0–0	No house. Farming in High Legh?
Barrymore, Earl of	Aston Park	114	100	100–0–0	For his son Hon. John Smith Barry and wife.
Beswick, William	Smithy at Arley Green	4	3½	3–10–0	Demolished. He was the blacksmith.
Birchall, Thomas	Cowhouse Farm and Arley Mill	240	120½	120–10–0	At Arley Green. This was the 16th/17th century home farm.
Chorton, Edward	Clockhouse	2	4½	4–10–0	He was a labourer on Arley farm (see Table 8).
Dewsbury, Samuel	at Feldy	1	½	12–6	See Appendix 2.2.
Dutton, Samuel	Gore Farm	192	70	55–10–0	See Appendix 1.
Glover, Samuel	by Hollin Hall	15	9½	9–10–0	See Appendix 2.2.
Houghton, Isaac	Cottage nr mill?	–	1½	1–10–0	Labourer in Arley Hall, earlier a small tenant farmer. See Table 8.
Hulme, James	Smaller Faulters, etc.	68	28	28–0–0	No house. Lived in Crowley where he was a tenant farmer.
Kinsey, Ralph	land on Cann Lane	68	32	32–0–0	No house. See Appendix 2.3, under Tovey.

Robinson, John	land nr Birchbrook	53	20	20–0–0	See Appendix 2.2. J. Walton took over when he died this year.
Starkey, James	land nr Hilltop	22	15	15–0–0	See Appendix 2.2.
	Total	1217	640		

APPENDIX 3 *A Note about Acreage and Maps*

The acreage figures used in Table 1 are derived from the eighteenth-century maps at Arley Hall and their reference books in WM Box 21; for Lymm and Pulford there are only survey figures, and for Marthall see note 4. The maps are very large and show the occupier and the acreage of every field. James Barfoot's modernised versions have been redrawn especially for this book by Denys Baker. The original maps show only Warburton lands, but James Barfoot and I have added data on other estates from a variety of sources, including the John Rylands University Library of Manchester (J.R.U.L.M.), Tabley estate maps; Cheshire Record Office (Cheshire R.O.), Appleton enclosure 1765, Appleton tithe award 1846. The Crowley map used here (p. 35) was created from several nineteenth-century maps at Arley Hall.

Notes:
1. T. S. Willan, *The Navigation of the River Weaver in the Eighteenth Century* (Chetham Soc., 3rd series, Vol. III, 1951), pp. 49–62.
2. Most of the Warburton muniments (WM) pre-1800 are deposited in J.R.U.L.M. I have catalogued these in great detail. The maps, private letters and a few items mostly of a decorative character are at Arley Hall where the author is the archivist. Almost every statement is derived from these papers. Box numbers are given only for important documents.
3. For the acreage figures see Appendix 3. For the income figures see WM Boxes 17–18; the detailed valuation of the home farm is from Appendix 1.
4. Cheshire R.O., Egerton of Tatton papers, DET.3229/31. Sir Peter Warburton sold the manor to Samuel Egerton of Tatton in 1745. This is Sir Peter's valuation of the manor, with tenants and their leases detailed.
5. For a discussion of the size and value of landed estates see G. E. Mingay, *English Landed Society in the Eighteenth Century* (London, 1963), and J. V. Beckett, *The Aristocracy of England* (London, 1986). For the wealth of the Booths see J. V. Beckett and C. Jones, 'Financial improvidence and political independence in the early eighteenth century: George Booth, 2nd Earl of Warrington (1675–1758)', *Bulletin J.R.U.L.M.*, LXV (1983).

6. Cheshire R.O., tithe maps and schedules 1846; WM Boxes 38–75, deeds.
7. National Westminster Bank PLC, *200 Years in Warrington 1788–1988* (Warrington, [1988]). The present Regional Office in Winwick Street was the head office of Parr's Bank.
8. WM Boxes 1–76. Almost every box has contributed something to building up the information in Appendix 2. The maps at Arley and other papers there are important. Leicester of Tabley papers at Cheshire R.O. and J.R.U.L.M. have been used for Appendices 2.3 and 2.6, but see note on Appendix 2.6. Tables 2 to 5 are based on Appendix 2. See also Appendix 1.
9. WM Boxes 10–18, 21, 25, 32, 35–6, 48–76.
10. WM Box 2.
11. *Arley Charters*, ed. W. Beamont (London, 1866). Originals in J.R.U.L.M.
12. Leicester-Warren of Tabley papers in Cheshire R.O. and J.R.U.L.M., only part catalogued or sorted.
13. WM Box 70, for Daniel family settlements. In 1758 the estate was broken up and distributed to the granddaughters. Sir Peter Warburton bought the land in Aston and Sir Peter Leicester that in Over Tabley.
14. See Appendix 1 for the rents received on this estate by Sir George Warburton in 1740.
15. WM Box 72, deeds of Brownslane/Belmont Estate 1723–1834.
16. J.R.U.L.M., Dunham Massey papers in process of being catalogued; WM Box 69.
17. WM Box 61 for Rutter.
18. Christ Church, Oxford, Archives: Great Budworth, Tithes Volume.
19. WM Box 2. His age is shown as 74 in the 1745 Abstract of Budworth leases, which has been used for all the ages in Appendix 2.5, but it may be inaccurate. He may have needed to be 21 and legally qualified to preside at his first manor court in 1689.
20. G. Ormerod, *History of Cheshire*, I; Cheshire R.O., Leigh of West Hall papers. This family is interesting at this period because their estate, though ancient, was not apparently able to support them in gentry style. One of their major assets was the right to appoint a rector of Lymm (probably worth about £200 p.a. in the 1740s). Using this as a base, four members of the family carved out successful clerical careers between 1698 and 1758. Egerton Leigh came down from Christ Church, Oxford, aged about 22, to his first job as curate of Great Budworth in 1724. The same year he inherited the estate. After his marriage, he and his wife lived with her father at Aston Park and had five children between 1725 and 1732.
21. Garland Hall was so named later in the eighteenth century from James Garland who was Hamlet Yate's tenant *c.* 1712–42.
22. Cheshire R.O., DET.3229/31.
23. WM Box 2 for E. Lawrence's report.
24. Matthew Lyon was active in the malt business and probably, as noted above, in partnership with the Rev. Thomas Moss in the malt kiln and brewery at Wilderspool. Matthew Lyon may also have been involved with a sugar refinery in Warrington. It was his son Thomas who was a founder partner of Parr's Bank in 1788 and whose descendants built Appleton Hall on the site of this farm and became one of the great squires of the area in the 19th century (WM Boxes 49–50, Lyon deeds).
25. WM Boxes 63 and 64, Moss deeds.
26. William Clayton's estate was divided among his five daughters. Three married Liverpool businessmen and one a Lancashire landowner. Sarah, the youngest, who never married, inherited the coal mines on the Parr Hall estate, Prescot, which she ran in partnership with her nephew Thomas Case. She also developed Clayton Square in Liverpool. So in this family there were not only leading merchants of Liverpool and Warrington, but substantial landowners in Lancashire and Cheshire: (WM Box 65; S. A. Harris, 'Sarah Clayton's letter and John Wood of Bath', *Transactions of the Historical*

Society of Lancashire and Cheshire (T.H.S.L.C.), C (1948), pp. 55–8.

27. Quaker registers of births, marriages and deaths at Friends' House Library, Euston Road, London.
28. WM Box 56 for Hough family deeds.
29. WM Box 62, Southern/Bate deeds.
30. Cheshire R.O., J. Vernon's will.
31. WM Box 70, Vernon deeds.
32. WM Boxes 71, 72, 74, Pimlow and Penny deeds.
33. WM Box 24, Folder 10, S. Glover's will, 1751.
34. WM Box 49, for Crowley freehold; J. Foster, *Alumni Oxonienses* (London, 1891 and 1887), for the Boardmans.
35. The problem is that we cannot trace descent through the female line in these papers because not enough leases have survived. There are certainly indications that more leases descended in families even in the eighteenth century than four out of thirty-two.
36. Cheshire R.O., will of R. Dewsbury, pr. 1751.
37. Cheshire R.O., will of O. Broom, pr. 1753.
38. Arley Hall, the Arley estate account book of Thomas Done 1750–4.
39. WM Box 19, Estate Accounts. Every year in the 1750s and 1760s he was paid for carriage to and from Chester. In 1763 when he and his wife were ill and she died, Sir Peter gave him a shilling a week for more than a year.
40. WM Box 26.
41. WM Vouchers. It is possible that Thomas Byfield, Sir Peter's man, was married. Thomas Done the accountant married Lady Elizabeth's maid Catherine Shuttleworth in 1751, when his salary was increased to £40 a year.
42. The maps at Arley Hall normally show two or three buildings at a farm and the Reference Books (Box 21) say 'House outbuildings, garden and orchard'. At a cottage a single building is usually shown and the Reference Book reads 'Cottage (or house) and garden'. In Great Budworth in some places where two buildings appear on the map the Reference Book says '2 houses and gardens'. I have counted one house at each map position unless I have other information. This appears to indicate that houses were shared by two families without a permanent division existing.
43. J.D. Marshall, *Autobiography of William Stout* (Chetham Society, 3rd series, vol. XIV, Manchester, 1967), pp. 90–123.
44. A. W. Boyd, 'The town books of Sevenoaks and Newton–by–Daresbury, Cheshire', *Transactions of the Lancashire and Cheshire Antiquarian Society (T.L.C.A.S.)*,, XLV (1928), p. 49.
45. WM Boxes 48–61 inclusive, for deeds of Crowley farms. The tax assessments of 1703 and 1749 in Box 25, and the lists of fee farm rents included with Crowley Lodge deeds in Boxes 53 and 54, were also useful in identifying tenants and owners.
46. The annual value of the land in Aston is shown in Table 3 as £1,580. Of this sum 61% was farmed by tenants and 39% by freeholders and leaseholders. The differences between this proportion and that of the numbers of farmers is mainly caused by the three very large rack rented farms on Arley demesne.
47. Cheshire R.O., will of T. Clare, pr. 1724. He marked this will.
48. For example, the high annual values of some properties in the area.
49. A member of another of the Eaton families of the area lived at 3 Dene Cottages in 1745. He was Mr Abdullah Eaton who died in 1755, when his heir was the Revd John Eaton, then a fellow of Brasenose College, who probably later retired to Great Budworth.
50. Mr Mills was the tenant of Ann Mee. The Mees were an important freeholder family in Over Peover, of which Richard Mee, gent, was the head in the 1730s. Samuel Mee was a mercer in Knutsford and Hugh Mee was vicar of Sandbach 1729–32. They

were closely related to Thomas Gorst, lawyer, of Middlewich, who was manager of the Tabley estate 1741–63. This gentry family, therefore, had a member in all four occupations: landowner, priest, businessman and lawyer.

51. Cheshire R.O., will of Alice Edwards, pr. 1759.
52. Cheshire R.O., Great Budworth parish book.
53. Cheshire R.O., wills and alehouse licences.
54. I hope to undertake a further study on the agriculture of this area from 1750 to 1790, which will examine the financial position of tenant farmers.
55. WM Box 25, Folder of tax assessments, gives the rates for runs of years in all four townships during the period 1750–75. Many of the gaps can be filled in from estate accounts and vouchers, particularly tenants' disbursement vouchers.
56. See Table 2, note 4.
57. J. D. Marshall, op.cit.
58. I hope to undertake a further study of the development of the Warburton estate in the eighteenth and nineteenth centuries.
59. *Land and Property: the English Land Tax, 1692–1832*, ed. D. R. Mills and M. E. Turner (Gloucester, 1986).
60. Ibid., pp. 180–8.

Index

This is an index of (1) townships; (2) houses which before 1770 had names other than that of the present or past occupier; and (3) people.